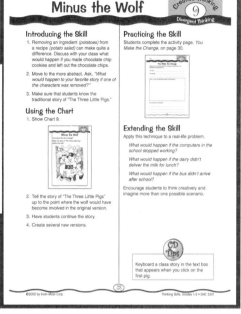

A **teacher page** that provides ideas for introducing the chart, step-by-step instructions for doing the chart activity, and suggestions for extending the skill introduced. Specific hints for interacting with the CD chart are included on this page as well.

A **chart** that poses a problem or question. Reproduce these charts on overhead transparencies for ease of presentation. Choose the lessons and the order of use that are appropriate to the needs of your students. Note that charts are presented with the simplest skills first, moving to more complex skills.

A reproducible **student page** to be used with the chart or as follow-up practice. Use as many reproducible practice pages as appropriate for your students. These pages may be used with the whole class or as independent practice.

An **Answer Key** for the charts and practice pages begins on page 139.

About the CD-ROM

Loading the Program

1 Put the CD in your CD drive.

This CD-ROM contains both Windows and MacOS programs.

Your computer will recognize the correct program.

2 On some computers, the program will automatically start up. If the program does not start automatically:

Windows—go to My Computer, double click on the CD drive, then double click on Begin.exe.

MacOS—double click on the CD icon on your desktop, then double click on Begin.

3 After the program starts, you will arrive at the main menu.

Main Menu Features

The 44 lessons found in the book are presented in full-color with an interactive element. To present a whole-class lesson, connect your computer to a projection system. As a review, students may be taught to access a specific lesson during their computer time.

○ **Choose a Topic**

1 Click on **Choose a Skill** to display the list of skills.

2 Click on a category. The category will be displayed, along with lesson numbers.

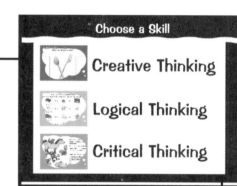

3 Click on a lesson number. The lesson will be displayed, followed by a full-color illustration of a lesson in the book. For example, **Lesson 1, Just a Pencil.**

4 Refer to the lesson in the workbook. For example, in Lesson 1 you can list the ways to use a pencil by clicking on the question mark in the box next to the image as directed in the CD Tips box in your workbook lesson.

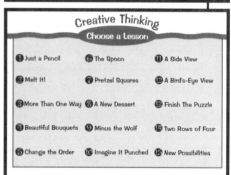

5 After listing and discussing the suggestions from the class, click on **Choose a Lesson** to select the next lesson number, and repeat steps 3 and 4.

6 You may click on **Choose a Skill** to select another category, or click on **Main Menu** and select **Exit** to close the program.

Thinking Skills, Grades 1–2 • EMC 5301

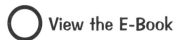 **View the E-Book**

- The charts, practice pages, and answer key are presented in a printable electronic format. You must have Adobe® Acrobat® Reader™ installed to access the e-book. (See installation instructions below.)

Installing Adobe® Acrobat® Reader™

You need to have Acrobat Reader installed on your computer to access the e-book portion of the CD-ROM. If you do not have Acrobat Reader, go to the main menu of the CD and follow these instructions:

1. Place your cursor over the Click Here link. Wait for the hand and then click.
2. When you see the Acrobat Reader Setup Screen, click the "Next" box.
3. When you see the Destination Location Screen, click the "Next" box.
4. When you see the Setup Complete Screen, click "finish."

Your system will now shut down to finish the installation process. Some systems will automatically restart. If yours does not, start it up manually.

- You may scroll through the entire book page by page or open the "Bookmarks" tab for a clickable table of contents.

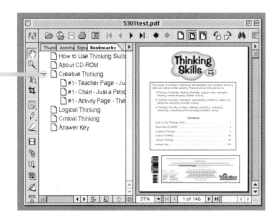

Hint: This symbol,⊞ for Windows or ▷ for MacOS, means that you can click there to expand the category.

- To print pages from the e-book, click on the printer icon. A print dialog box will open. Enter the page or pages you wish to print in the print range boxes. (At the bottom of the screen, you can see which page of the e-book you are viewing.)

- To exit the e-book, simply "X" out until you return to the main menu.

Exit This button closes the program.

Thinking Skills, Grades 1–2 • EMC 5301

Creative Thinking

Thinking Skills, Grades 1–2 • EMC 5301

Just a Pencil

Introducing the Skill

1. Introduce the term **brainstorming**.

   Brainstorming is an important part of shared problem solving. It is simply generating as many ideas as possible that address a specific topic or problem. The American industrialist Alex Osbourne coined the expression in the 1950s. He outlined ways to generate many innovative ideas and to build up healthy group dynamics.

2. Give students the following brainstorming guidelines and monitor brainstorming sessions to ensure that the rules are followed.

   • All ideas are valuable. *(Don't judge or evaluate ideas during the brainstorming process.)*

   • It's good to build on someone else's idea.

   • Unusual ideas are welcome.

Using the Chart

1. Show the chart to the students. Begin with the simple question about the familiar object on Chart 1—the pencil.

2. With students, brainstorm the different ways a pencil could be used.

3. Record **all** the ideas.

Practicing the Skill

Students complete the activity page, *The Marvelous Milk Carton,* on page 7. They will be generating new ideas about another familiar object.

Extending the Skill

After generating ideas, move to classifying and evaluating as your students' levels of readiness allow.

   • Combine ideas that are the same.

   • Group ideas in categories.

   • Evaluate the ideas as possible for your students or impossible.

CD Tips

Click in the text box and keyboard the list of ideas.

(5)

Just a Pencil

How many uses can you think of for a pencil?

List as many as you can.

The Marvelous Milk Carton

How many ways can you use a milk carton?

Draw or write your ideas on the carton.

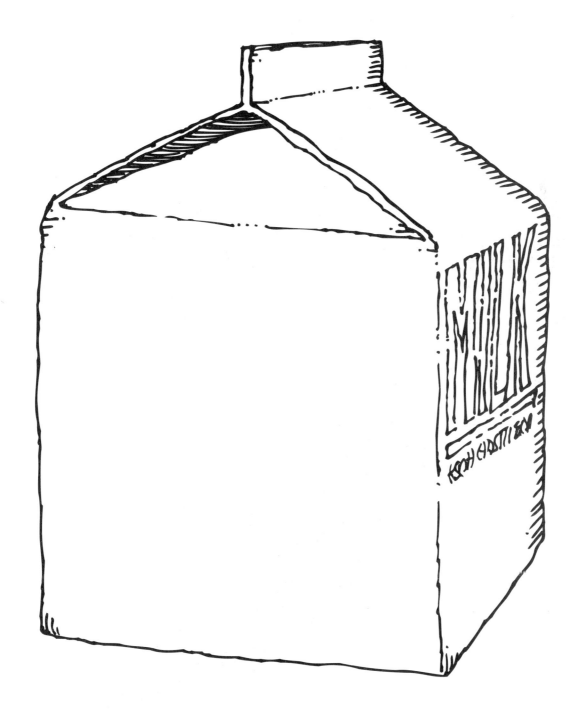

Melt It!

Introducing the Skill

Help your students to realize that there are many ways to accomplish most tasks by giving an example. Try to personalize the example so that it is a part of your students' experiences.

I've noticed that after lunch, different classes get their lunch boxes back to their rooms in different ways. Mrs. Kehl's room has a tub. When the students are finished eating lunch, they put their lunch boxes in the tub. After lunch, Mr. Ruiz brings the tub to their room. Mrs. Bennett's students put their lunch boxes just outside their door as they go out for lunch recess. Mrs. Johnson's students line up their lunch boxes along the playground fence. Then they pick them up after recess. Have you noticed any other ways?

Using the Chart

1. Show Chart 2.

2. Have students think of at least five ways to melt an ice cube.

3. Record the responses on the chalkboard or a chart.

Practicing the Skill

Students independently complete the activity page, *Getting Down,* on page 10.

Extending the Skill

Encourage your students to consider options to more everyday occurrences. Assign a quota of ideas to fill. This will promote mental flexibility.

- Think of five different ways to take all of your library books to the library.

- Think of five ways that we can let the custodian know that we appreciate his work.

Click in each box and keyboard possible solutions. Don't limit possibilities to five. Each box may have one or more solutions.

Thinking Skills, Grades 1–2 • EMC 5301

Melt It!

Think of five ways to melt an ice cube.

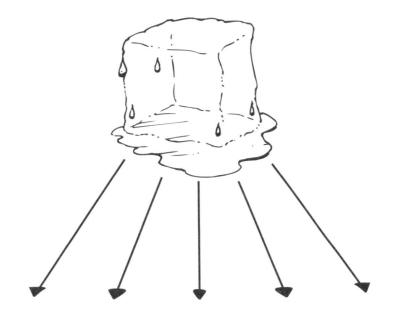

?	?	?	?	?

Getting Down

Think of four ways to get down from a slide.

Draw or write one way in each box.

?	?	?	?

Thinking Skills, Grades 1–2 • EMC 5301

Introducing the Skill

1. Bring a stuffed animal to class. Ask students to think of different ways to carry the animal.

2. Record the suggestions on the chalkboard or a chart.

Using the Chart

1. Show Chart 3.

2. Give students a sheet of paper. Each student should select a pet. They draw the pet at the top of the page.

3. Then students think of at least two ways to carry the pet. They draw each of the ways under the pet.

4. Allow time to share students' ideas.

Practicing the Skill

Students complete the activity page, *Getting the Job Done,* on page 13. Each student will identify a job and think of at least two ways to do the job.

Extending the Skill

1. Emphasize the importance of considering different possibilities and trying them out. Have students try the suggestions recorded on the chalkboard for carrying the stuffed animal.

2. Evaluate the ideas. Decide which way was the most efficient, the quickest, the most fun, or the easiest. You may discover helpful new ways of doing things.

Click on the animals to see special requirements that need to be considered when designing a carrier.

Fish—I'll need water.

Bird—I'll get sick if I'm cold or wet.

Big cat—I can climb out of almost anything.

Big dog—I'm really heavy!

Little cat—I'm afraid to leave my mom.

Little pup—I like to chew things.

Thinking Skills, Grades 1–2 • EMC 5301

More Than One Way

Think of at least two ways to carry your pet.

Getting the Job Done

Decide on a job. Then think of at least two ways to do it.

Draw or write your job idea here.

Draw or write two ways to do the job below.

1

2

Beautiful Bouquets

Introducing the Skill

1. Use real things to introduce the idea that there is more than one possible combination of items in a set.

   Show a banana, a sandwich, juice, and a cookie.

2. Say, *"I can take three things in my lunch."* Ask, *"Which three should I take?"*

3. Record student suggestions on the chalkboard or a chart.

Using the Chart

1. Show Chart 4.

2. Tell students that each flower may be used only once in each bouquet. Have students suggest different combinations of flowers.

3. Record the responses. You may want to reproduce the flower squares *(three of each flower)* and actually arrange them in the combinations suggested. There are four possible bouquets.

Practicing the Skill

Students complete the activity page, *Color-It Combinations,* on page 16. There are six possible combinations for responses to the activity page challenge if the colors are used only once in each combination.

Extending the Skill

Have students discover how the number of possible combinations changes when two, three, or four flowers in a bunch are the same color. Have students share the strategies they used to find the different combinations.

Make the four possible bouquets. Click on the flower and drag it to a vase. Repeat with different flowers.

Thinking Skills, Grades 1–2 • EMC 5301

Beautiful Bouquets

What different bouquets can you make using these flowers? Use only three flowers in each bouquet.

tulip
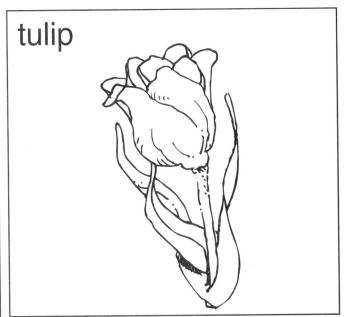

daisy

iris
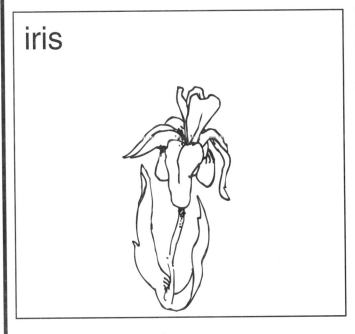

lily
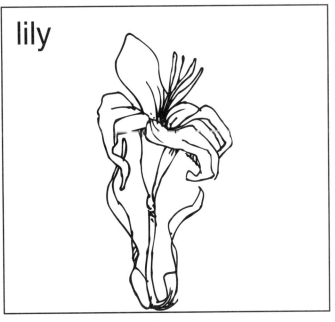

Color-It Combinations

What different ways can you color the flowers?

Use only red, purple, green, orange, blue, and yellow crayons.

Each flower may be only one color. Each flower in a set must be a different color.

Thinking Skills, Grades 1–2 • EMC 5301

Change the Order

Introducing the Skill

Propose a "what if?" question that draws on your students' experiences.

What if we took the spelling test before we studied the words?

What if we tried to write with our pencils before we sharpened them?

Using the Chart

1. Show Chart 5.

2. With students, answer the what if's on the chart.

3. Ask, *"Is there a certain order in which you do some things?"*

Practicing the Skill

1. Students complete the activity page, *What If?*, on page 19.

2. Share students' work.

Extending the Skill

Ask students if order always matters. Ask them to give an example of a task where order doesn't matter.

Watering the garden—I can water the rows in different ways, and as long as I water every row, the order I water them in doesn't matter.

Washing the car—It doesn't matter whether I start at the front or the back. It does matter if I put the soap on after I rinse the car.

Click on the bullet to focus on a single what if.

Thinking Skills, Grades 1–2 • EMC 5301

Change the Order

Sometimes things need to be done in a certain order. Consider these "what if's."

- **What if** you put on your shoes and then your socks?

- **What if** you buttered the bread before you toasted it?

- **What if** you cast out your line before you put the bait on the hook?

- **What if** you cooked the egg before you cracked it?

What If?

Make up your own "what if." Then show what would happen.

The Spoon

Introducing the Skill

1. Bring a collection of different spoons into the classroom.

2. Ask students, *"What do we call these tools? Are they all used for the same purpose?"*

Using the Chart

1. Show Chart 6.

2. With students, brainstorm the different ways spoons are used. Ask, *"What jobs does a spoon do?"*

3. Record the responses.

Practicing the Skill

1. Encourage students to think divergently about the responses for Chart 6. For example:

   A spoon scoops.
   Ask, "How many different ways can you use the spoon to scoop?"

   A spoon scoops cantaloupe.

   A spoon scoops ice cream.

   A spoon scoops sand.

2. Repeat for each initial response.

Extending the Skill

Students complete the activity page, *What Does It Do?,* on page 22.

Click in the text box and keyboard students' responses.

Pretzel Squares

Introducing the Skill

Students love a challenge! Explain to students that you will be giving each of them 12 stick pretzels. These are to be used to solve the problem. After the lesson, you may want to give out clean pretzels as a snack.

Using the Chart

1. Show Chart 7.

2. Read the problem to your students.

3. As your students begin forming squares, encourage them to think divergently. They may at first simply form three squares, using four pretzels for each square. Help them see that by connecting the squares they can form more. Looking at something in a new way is a very important part of thinking creatively.

4. Have students share their solutions by dragging the pretzels into squares, drawing them on the chalkboard, or laying their pretzels on a lighted overhead projector.

Practicing the Skill

1. Give each student nine drinking straws for the activity page.

2. Students use the straws to make triangles on their desktops and then draw the triangles to complete the activity page, *How Many Triangles?*, on page 25.

Click and drag the pretzels into squares. Use only twelve.

Pretzel Squares

Use 12 pretzels to make as many squares as you can. Try several different ways. What is the largest number you made?

Minus the Wolf

Introducing the Skill

1. Removing an ingredient *(potatoes)* from a recipe *(potato salad)* can make quite a difference. Discuss with your class what would happen if you made chocolate chip cookies and left out the chocolate chips.

2. Move to the more abstract. Ask, *"What would happen to your favorite story if one of the characters was removed?"*

3. Make sure that students know the traditional story of "The Three Little Pigs."

Using the Chart

1. Show Chart 9.

2. Tell the story of "The Three Little Pigs" up to the point where the wolf would have become involved in the original version.

3. Have students continue the story.

4. Create several new versions.

Practicing the Skill

Students complete the activity page, *You Make the Change,* on page 31.

Extending the Skill

Apply this technique to a real-life problem.

What would happen if the computers in the school stopped working?

What would happen if the dairy didn't deliver the milk for lunch?

What would happen if the bus didn't arrive after school?

Encourage students to think creatively and imagine more than one possible scenario.

Keyboard a class story in the text box that appears when you click on the first pig.

29

Minus the Wolf

How would the story change?

Retell the story of "The Three Little Pigs" without the wolf.

Imagine It Punched

Sally folded a piece of paper in half and punched the hole with a hole punch.

What will the paper look like when Sally unfolds it?

Imagine It Unfolded

Draw to show what each paper will look like when it is unfolded.

1

2

3

4

Thinking Skills, Grades 1–2 • EMC 5301

A Side View

Introducing the Skill

1. This exercise asks students to visualize the side of a symmetrical block building. If your students are not familiar with the term **symmetrical**, explain that it means that something is exactly the same on both sides. (*If you are looking at the front of a building, the back will be exactly the same.*)

2. Set up a symmetrical stack of blocks.

3. Have students tell what the stack would look like from the side.

4. Check to see if predictions are correct.

Using the Chart

1. Show Chart 11.

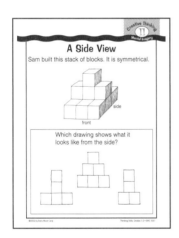

2. Have students select one drawing from the chart to answer the question.

3. Confirm perceptions by using real blocks to build the figure. View it from the side and compare it to student drawings.

Practicing the Skill

1. Students complete the activity page, *Around the Corner,* on page 37.

2. Build the wooden block structures to check predictions.

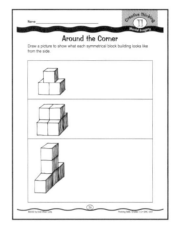

Extending the Skill

Build a block structure. Have students draw what it looks like from each side and above and below.

Click on the block pattern to make it rotate.

Thinking Skills, Grades 1–2 • EMC 5301

A Side View

Sam built this stack of blocks. It is symmetrical.

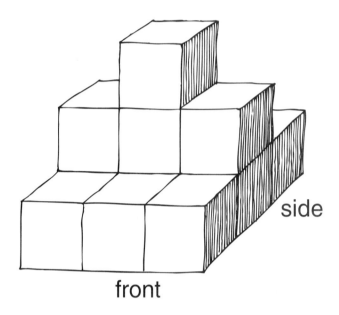

side

front

Which drawing shows what it looks like from the side?

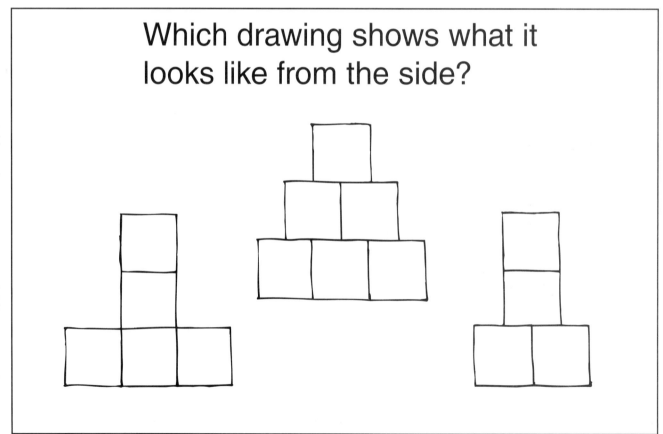

Around the Corner

Draw a picture to show what each symmetrical block building looks like from the side.

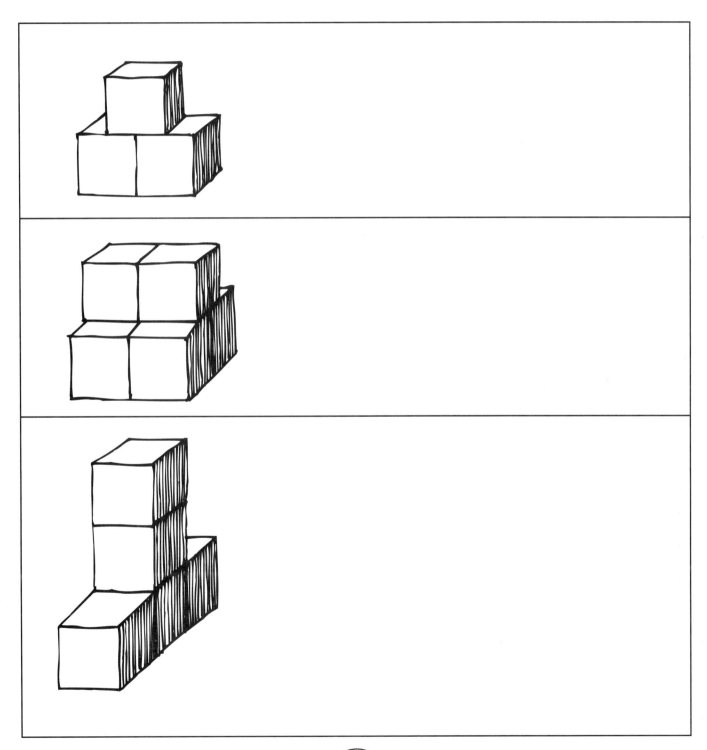

A Bird's-Eye View

Introducing the Skill

1. Ask students to view and describe a common classroom object *(jar of paste, pencil can, book)* at eye level. Encourage them to note the shape and size.

2. Have students view and describe the same object from above. They should note any differences in shape and size.

Using the Chart

1. Show Chart 12.

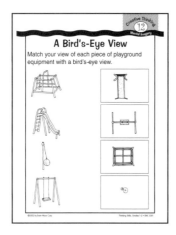

2. Have students match the equipment with the correct bird's-eye views.

3. Have students point out matching parts of different views.

Practicing the Skill

Students complete the activity page, *Flying Over,* on page 40.

Extending the Skill

1. Discuss the view seen from an airplane window. Ask, *"How do things look different than they do on the ground?"*

2. Locate and show a bird's-eye view of a real building—a photo taken from an airplane.

3. Have students take photos of several common objects from two different perspectives. Display the photos along with written descriptions.

Click on each piece of equipment to see the correct bird's-eye view.

Thinking Skills, Grades 1–2 • EMC 5301

A Bird's-Eye View

Match your view of each piece of playground equipment with a bird's-eye view.

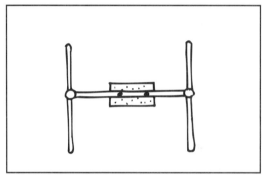

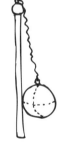

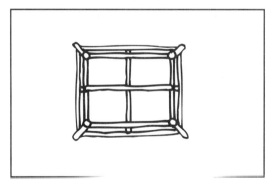

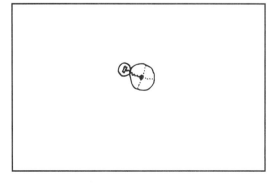

Flying Over

Draw to show what each object would look like from above.

| baseball field | swimming pool |
| big rig truck | apartment house |

Finish the Puzzle

Introducing the Skill

1. Have students put several picture puzzles together.

2. Now help your students to visualize the relationship of a part to the whole. This activity asks students to move beyond putting actual picture puzzles together. It asks them to put the pieces together in their heads.

Using the Chart

1. Show Chart 13.

2. Help students describe the components of each small square.

3. Ask leading questions such as,

   Do those lines look like they would be part of the _____ or the _____?

   or

   Where do you see the same shape in the large picture?

4. Have students give the row and column number of the proper location for each puzzle piece.

Practicing the Skill

Students complete the activity page, *Putting It Together,* on page 43.

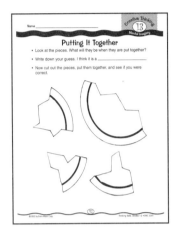

Extending the Skill

1. Choose a simple picture.

2. Cut the picture into 4 or 5 parts. Arrange the parts in random order.

3. Have students describe the picture.

4. Put the picture together to check the descriptions.

CD Tips

Click and drag the puzzle pieces to the correct positions.

Thinking Skills, Grades 1–2 • EMC 5301

Finish the Puzzle

Each small square is a piece of the big picture.
Can you figure out where each piece should be?

	A	B	C	D
1				
2				
3				
4				

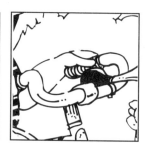

Putting It Together

- Look at the pieces. What will they be when they are put together?

- Write down your guess. I think it is a _____.

- Now cut out the pieces, put them together, and see if you were correct.

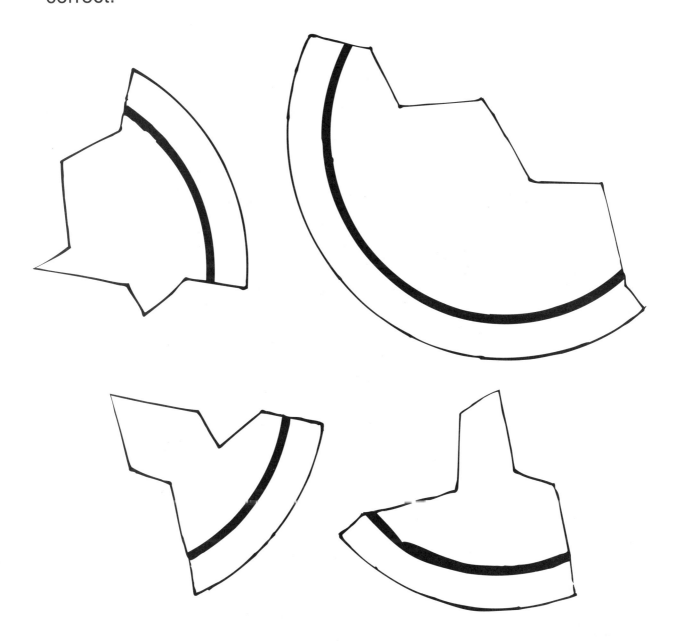

Thinking Skills, Grades 1–2 • EMC 5301

Two Rows of Four

Introducing the Skill

This activity is a brainteaser. It stretches your mind just as exercise stretches your body. Encourage your students to look at each brainteaser in many different ways to "loosen" their perception of it and see a solution.

Using the Chart

1. Show Chart 14.

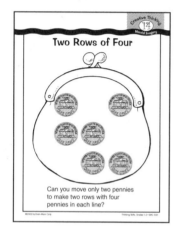

2. Have individual students look at the chart and imagine possible solutions.

3. Pass out real pennies or counting disks for manipulation.

4. Have students arrange disks on the overhead projector screen to display their solutions.

5. Ask students, *"What gave you the idea to look at the problem in a different way?"*

Practicing the Skill

Students complete the activity page, *Look Again,* on page 46.

Extending the Skill

Students write the entire alphabet using the mirror image pattern on the activity page.

Click and drag the pennies into two rows.

Two Rows of Four

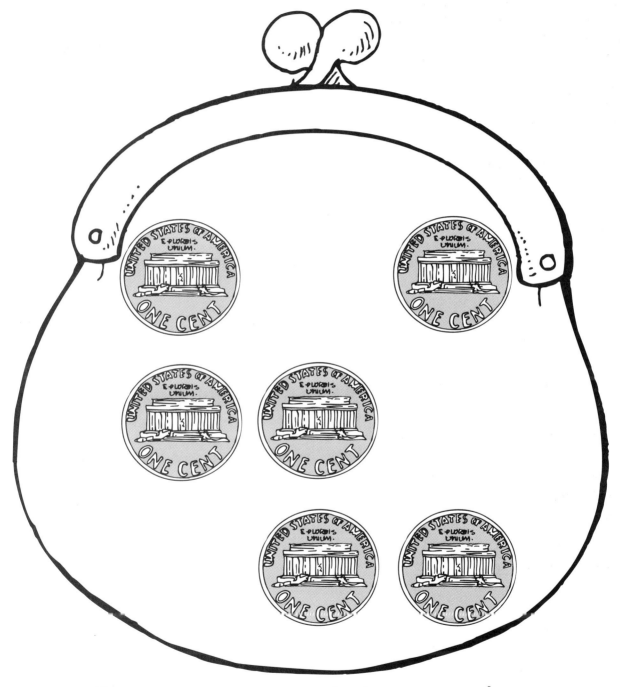

Can you move only two pennies
to make two rows with four
pennies in each line?

Look Again

What is the next shape in this sequence?

1 ꝏ	4 ꝺb
2 bd	5 ꝫꝫ
3 ꝏ	6

Thinking Skills, Grades 1–2 • EMC 5301

New Possibilities

Introducing the Skill

Imagining is part of thinking creatively. Students should be encouraged to imagine and then think of multiple answers to questions and problems.

Using the Chart

1. Show Chart 15.

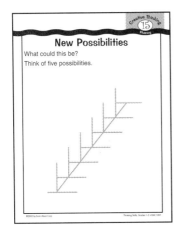

2. Encourage your students to look at the unusual shape from several different perspectives.

   - *Actually turn the paper.*

   - *Imagine the figure as giant-size. Then imagine it as microscopic.*

   - *How could it be used in a kitchen? A factory? A garage?*

3. Require each student to think of more than one possible answer.

Practicing the Skill

Students complete the activity page, *What's It For?*, on page 49.

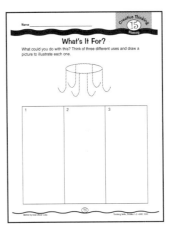

Extending the Skill

Students write an instruction manual for how to use the unusual shape for one of the purposes they have imagined.

Click in the box to record possible purposes.

New Possibilities

What could this be?

Think of five possibilities.

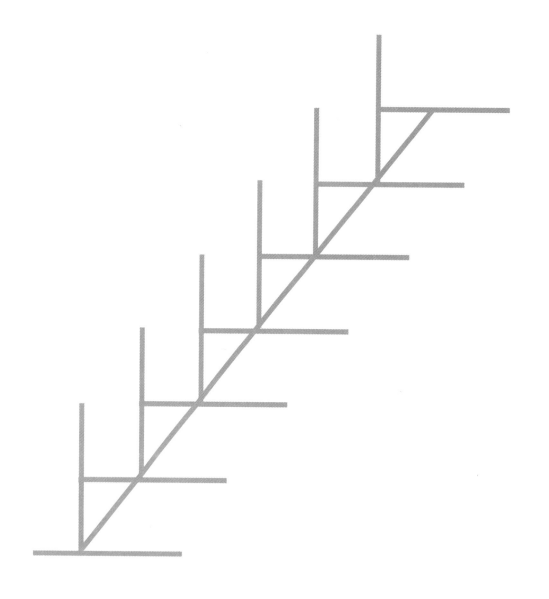

What's It For?

What could you do with this? Think of three different uses and draw a picture to illustrate each one.

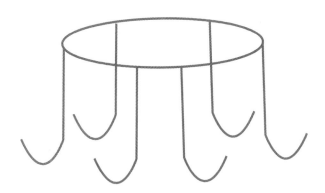

1	2	3

Thinking Skills, Grades 1–2 • EMC 5301

Logical Thinking

Thinking Skills, Grades 1–2 • EMC 5301

What's the Relationship?

Introducing the Skill

1. Have students explain what "making a comparison" means.

2. Introduce the term **analogy**. Explain that an analogy is a special kind of comparison. It compares two sets of things.

    An analogy is a formal comparison of the relationship between two sets of objects.

    The objects are different, but the relationships are the same. An analogy always follows this form:

    _____ *is to* _____ *as* _____ *is to* _____.

Using the Chart

1. Show Chart 1.

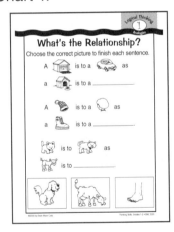

2. Guide the students through each analogy on the chart. Say:

    Let's name the pictures we see: garage, car, doghouse.

    Now let's read the first analogy.

    A garage is to a car as a doghouse is to a _____?

    Think about how a garage goes with a car.

That's right, a car goes in a garage; a garage is like a house for a car. What goes in a doghouse?

Practicing the Skill

Students complete the activity page, *Complete the Analogy,* on page 53.

Extending the Skill

Have students describe the relationship between the two sets of things compared in the analogies. Learning to look for the relationship will help students solve and write analogies.

CD Tips

Click and drag the correct picture to complete each analogy.

51

What's the Relationship?

Choose the correct picture to finish each sentence.

A  is to a  as

a  is to a _____.

A is to a as

a is to a _____.

 is to  as

 is to _____.

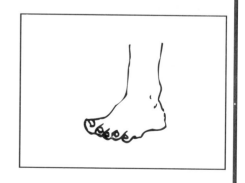

Complete the Analogy

Circle the picture that completes the analogy.

 is to as

is to _____.

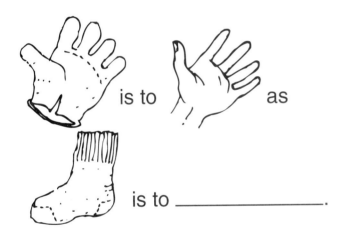 is to as

is to _____.

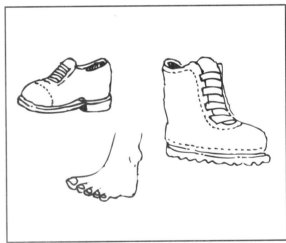

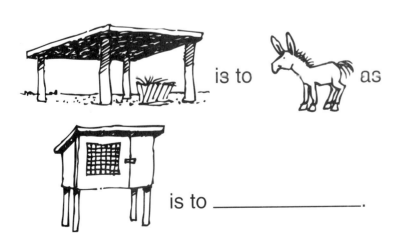 is to as

is to _____.

53

Make Your Own Analogies

Introducing the Skill

1. Remind students that in an analogy the relationships must be the same, but the subject will be different. Then help students set up a procedure for making their own analogies.

   • Identify the relationship. For example:
     ingredient—finished product

   • Think of sets of items that have that relationship.
     slice of bread—sandwich
     ice cream—sundae
     flour—cake

   • Follow the analogy format and insert two of the sets of items.
     Ice cream is to a sundae as flour is to a cake.

2. Brainstorm and list other possible relationships.

   place (bear : den :: bee : hive)

   numerical (5 : 10 :: 3 : 6)

   opposites (go : stop :: day : night)

   object-to-action (ear : hear :: eye : see)

   part-to-whole (wing : airplane :: wheel : wagon)

   sequence or degree (tiny : small :: big : gigantic)

Using the Chart

1. Show Chart 2.

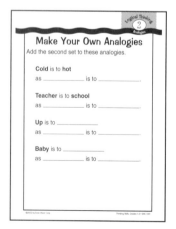

2. Work with students to identify the relationship, brainstorm other sets with the same relationship, and create a new analogy.

Practicing the Skill

Students complete the activity page, *My Analogy,* on page 56.

Extending the Skill

Give the first part of the analogy and have each student finish the analogy in a different way. Bind the pages together to make a class booklet.

Click on the blanks and keyboard names of objects to complete the analogies.

54

Make Your Own Analogies

Add the second set to these analogies.

Cold is to **hot**

as _____ is to _____.

Teacher is to **school**

as _____ is to _____.

Up is to _____

as _____ is to _____.

Baby is to _____

as _____ is to _____.

Hammer is to _____

as _____ is to _____.

My Analogy

Write your own analogy. Draw pictures to show the relationship.

_____ is to _____

as _____ is to _____.

Find the Pet Owners

Introducing the Skill

1. Familiarize yourself with matrix logic puzzles.

   *Start by gathering information from the clues. Use the matrix (chart) to keep track of the facts that you gather. Mark the boxes with **X** for **no**. Write **yes** in the answer box. Only one box in each row and column can have a **yes**.*

2. Tell your class you are going to show them a new way to solve a mystery.

Using the Chart

1. Show Chart 3.

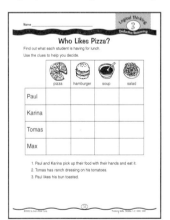

2. Read the question posed at the top together and then work carefully through each clue. Practice marking the squares in response to the information that you gather. Here is the reasoning for the pet puzzle on the chart:

   ### Clue 1: Sally loves her kitten.
   The clue tells the reader that Sally has a kitten, so write *yes* in the square under kitten, opposite Sally's name. *X* all the other squares under kitten because no two children have the same pet. Also, Sally has only one pet, so put an *X* in all the other boxes in her row.

   ### Clue 2: Sam is allergic to pet hair.
   Since Sam is allergic to pet hair, his pet must be hairless. Put an *X* under puppy and goat, opposite Sam's name. So Sam has either the lizard or the canary.

Clue 3: Susie hates reptiles.
If Susie hates reptiles she would not have a lizard for a pet. Put an *X* in the box under lizard and across from Susie's name.

Clue 4: Sara's pet sits on a perch.
Sara must have a canary. Put *yes* under canary, opposite Sara's name. Put an *X* in the other boxes under canary (to show that no one else has a canary) and opposite Sara (to show that she has no other pet).

Clue 5: Sean feeds his pet grass and hay.
Sean must have a goat. Mark the matrix. Look over the matrix carefully. You will be able to complete it now. There is only one box left for each person. Recall that Sam is allergic to pet hair and Susie hates reptiles, so Susie must have a puppy and Sam, a lizard.

Practicing the Skill

Students complete the activity page, *Who Likes Pizza?,* on page 59. Depending on your students' level, do the worksheet as a class, in small groups, or independently.

CD Tips

Drag an *X* or a *yes* into each section of the grid.

Thinking Skills, Grades 1–2 • EMC 5301

Find the Pet Owners

Sally, Sam, Susie, Sara, and Sean have pets. No two have the same pet. Use the clues to help you tell which pet each child has.

	kitten	lizard	puppy	canary	goat
Sara					
Susie					
Sally					
Sam					
Sean					

1. Sally loves her kitten.

2. Sam is allergic to pet hair.

3. Susie hates reptiles.

4. Sara's pet sits on a perch.

5. Sean feeds his pet grass and hay.

Who Likes Pizza?

Find out what each student is having for lunch.

Use the clues to help you decide.

	pizza	hamburger	soup	salad
Paul				
Karina				
Tomas				
Max				

1. Paul and Karina pick up their food with their hands and eat it.

2. Tomas has ranch dressing on his tomatoes.

3. Paul likes his bun toasted.

Piano Lessons

Introducing the Skill

1. Review with students when to put an *X* and when to put a *yes* on the matrix logic puzzle.

2. Remind students that there can be only one *yes* in each row and column.

Using the Chart

1. Show Chart 4.

2. Read the chart together.

3. Model gathering the information and responding to it appropriately.

4. Solve the puzzle together.

   Clue 1: Andre and Kim don't play for Mrs. Andersen on Thursday or Friday. Put an *X* under both Thursday and Friday for Andre and Kim.

   Clue 2: Steve and Carlos don't go to lessons on Wednesday, but Maya does. Put a *yes* opposite Maya's name under Wednesday. Put an *X* in the other boxes in the column and row.

   Clue 3: Kim goes the day before Andre. Andre and Kim must have lessons on Monday and Tuesday. Since Kim goes the day before Andre, Kim has lessons on Monday, and Andre has lessons on Tuesday. Put *yes* and *X* where appropriate.

Clue 4: Carlos goes the day after Steve. Since only Thursday and Friday are available, and Carlos goes the day after Steve, his lesson must be on Friday. Steve must have lessons on Thursday. Put *yes* and *X* where appropriate.

Practicing the Skill

Depending on your students' level, do the worksheet, *At the Zoo*, on page 62, as a class, in small groups, or independently.

Drag an *X* or a *yes* into each section of the grid.

Thinking Skills, Grades 1–2 • EMC 5301

Piano Lessons

Mrs. Andersen gives one piano lesson each weekday after school. Andre, Kim, Steve, Maya, and Carlos take lessons. Tell on what days the students have their lessons.

	Monday	Tuesday	Wednesday	Thursday	Friday
Andre					
Kim					
Steve					
Maya					
Carlos					

1. Andre and Kim don't play for Mrs. Andersen on Thursday or Friday.

2. Steve and Carlos don't go to lessons on Wednesday, but Maya does.

3. Kim goes the day before Andre.

4. Carlos goes the day after Steve.

At the Zoo

The Sutter family (Dad, Mom, Jamal, and Tenisha) went to the zoo. Each family member liked a different animal best. Use the clues and the matrix to find out what animals the family members chose as their favorites.

Dad				
Mom				
Tenisha				
Jamal				

1. Jamal's favorite was the heaviest animal.

2. Mom's favorite animal nibbled leaves off the tree.

3. Tenisha's favorite animal hung from a branch.

Thinking Skills, Grades 1–2 • EMC 5301

Where Do They Sit?

Introducing the Skill

1. Set up a table and four chairs—one chair on each side of the table.

2. On the chalkboard or a chart, draw a diagram showing the table.

3. Have a student sit in each chair. Write the names of the students on the diagram. This will help students see the relation between the diagram and the actual table and people in chairs. Explain to students that positions may be rotated, but the order must be the same.

Using the Chart

1. Show Chart 5.

2. Give four students name tags that match the four names in the puzzle. Enact the puzzle as you solve it together.

3. Read and analyze each clue in order. Here is the reasoning with questions to ask to help students begin their analysis:

Clue 1: The first word formed is BALL. Who has the letters to spell BALL? Kirk does, so he must have played first. Have the student wearing Kirk's name tag choose any chair and sit. Write the name *Kirk* in the same location on the chart to show where he is sitting.

Clue 2: Next, a player spells LOOK. Since the only letter in BALL that matches LOOK is L, the next player must have built the word LOOK from the L. Who has the letters OOK? Laurie does. Have the student wearing Laurie's name tag sit beside Kirk. Since play moves to the left, she must sit on Kirk's left. Write Laurie's name on the chart in the appropriate spot.

Clue 3: ZOOM is the next word. Figure out where the word ZOOM could be added to the game. It fits on the second O in LOOK. So the player who made the word must have the letters ZOM. Since Rosa has those letters, she must be the next player. The student wearing Rosa's name tag should sit on Laurie's left. Write Rosa's name in the appropriate box on the chart. Then the student wearing Lon's name tag must sit in the fourth chair.

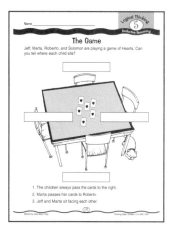

Practicing the Skill

Students complete the activity page, *The Game,* on page 65. This page may be done as a class project or individually.

CD Tips

Drag a name onto a chair to show where each player is sitting.

Thinking Skills, Grades 1–2 • EMC 5301

Where Do They Sit?

Players have seven letters.

Play moves to the left.

Kirk draws	Laurie draws
BAWLLIT	PONOKMA
Lon draws	Rosa draws
BILOPOZ	SZOMAUD

1. The first word formed is BALL.

2. Next, a player spells LOOK.

3. ZOOM is the next word.

The Game

Jeff, Marta, Roberto, and Solomon are playing a game of Hearts. Can you tell where each child sits?

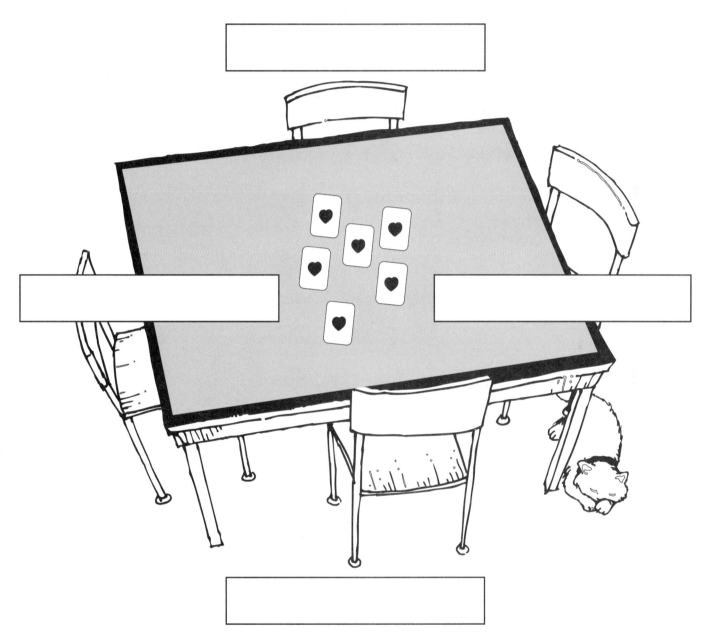

1. The children always pass the cards to the right.

2. Marta passes her cards to Roberto.

3. Jeff and Marta sit facing each other.

(65)

What Comes Next?

Introducing the Skill

Pattern is the underlying theme of mathematics. Recognizing and using patterns are important tools in problem solving. Students in primary classrooms need to experience patterns visually, auditorily, and physically.

Auditory patterning—*clap, clap, snap*

Physical patterning—*step, step, hop*

Visual patterning—◯ ◯ ▢

1. Provide experiences that allow your students to analyze, duplicate, and extend patterns with real things.

2. Move to symbolic representations of the same patterns before working with the chart.

Using the Chart

1. Show Chart 6.

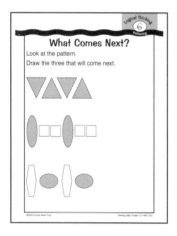

2. Have students read the pattern, giving a name to each of the symbols.

3. Extend the patterns.

Practicing the Skill

Students complete the activity page, *Continue the Pattern,* on page 68.

Extending the Skill

Note patterns in the way that you and your students move through the day.

Click and drag symbols to continue the patterns.

Thinking Skills, Grades 1–2 • EMC 5301

What Comes Next?

Look at the pattern.

Draw the three that will come next.

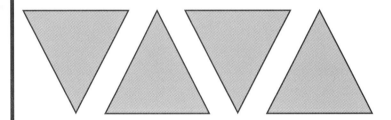

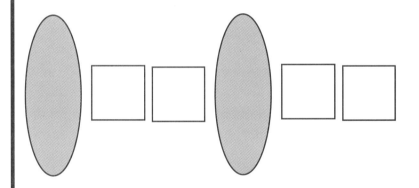

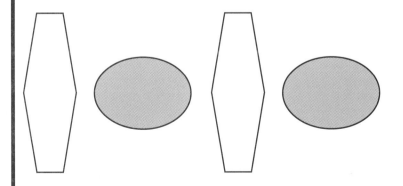

Continue the Pattern

Draw the next three items in each pattern.

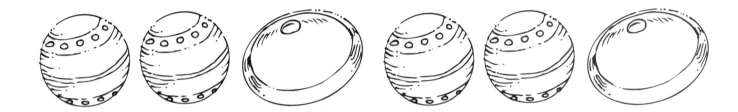

_____ _____ _____

_____ _____ _____

_____ _____ _____

Thinking Skills, Grades 1–2 • EMC 5301

Giving Patterns a Code

Introducing the Skill

Students need a code for describing and analyzing patterns. The letters of the alphabet make an easy code for young students.

1. Discuss what a code is. Explain that patterns can have a code or name.

2. Clap and snap a pattern *(snap clap snap clap)*.

3. Have students repeat the same pattern.

4. Ask students to use other objects to make the same pattern.

   red, blue, red, blue
   boy, girl, boy, girl
   pencil, paper, pencil, paper

5. Explain that these patterns have the same code—ABAB.

   A stands for one action, sound, or object.

   B stands for another action, sound, or object.

   If a third action, sound, or object is used, it is called C.

6. Show different AB patterns and have students name the patterns. Repeat until your students are comfortable with the process. Help students to generalize that there are many ABAB patterns.

Using the Chart

1. Show Chart 7.

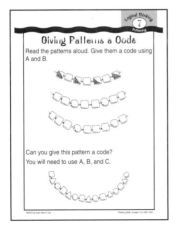

2. Work with students to name the patterns.

Practicing the Skill

Students complete the activity page, *Match Them*, on page 71.

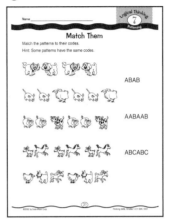

Extending the Skill

1. Give a pattern code at the beginning of the day.

   ABCABC

2. Have students identify examples of that pattern throughout the day.

Click in each bead and keyboard a letter to name the pattern.

Giving Patterns a Code

Read the patterns aloud. Give them a code using A and B.

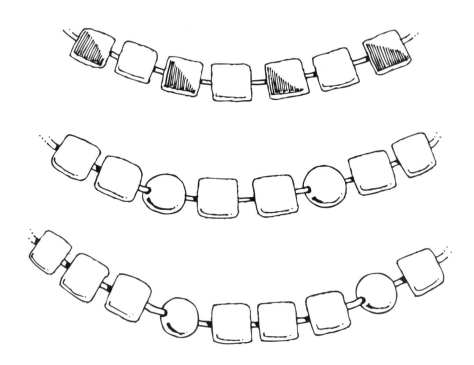

Can you give this pattern a code?

You will need to use A, B, and C.

Match Them

Match the patterns to their codes.

Hint: Some patterns have the same codes.

ABAB

AABAAB

ABCABC

Thinking Skills, Grades 1–2 • EMC 5301

How Many Patterns?

Introducing the Skill

1. Remind students that many different patterns can have the same code.

2. Explain that a single pattern can have more than one code as well.

   Example:
   blue square, blue circle, red square, blue circle, blue square, red circle

   One code:
   blue = A
   red = B   *AABAAB*

   Another code:
   square = A
   circle = B   *ABAB*

Using the Chart

1. Show Chart 8.

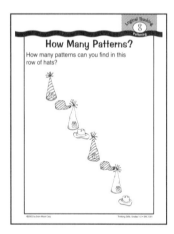

2. Challenge students to identify multiple codes for the pattern shown. Encourage them to look beyond the obvious by asking leading questions such as:

   Do some of the hats have similar designs or markings?

   Is there anything about the size of the hats that repeats a pattern?

   What can you say about the types of hats you see?

Practicing the Skill

Students complete the activity page, *Lunch Box Patterns,* on page 74.

Extending the Skill

Provide other multiple-code patterns and have students identify the codes.

Click in the text box and keyboard words to describe the pattern. Give each pattern a code.

Thinking Skills, Grades 1–2 • EMC 5301

How Many Patterns?

How many patterns can you find in this row of hats?

Lunch Box Patterns

Name three different patterns that you see in this set of lunch boxes.

  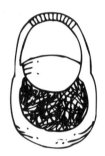   

Pattern 1	Pattern 2	Pattern 3

Make a Pattern

Introducing the Skill

Your students have been using letters to name patterns. Now ask them to create patterns that match the pattern code you provide. Begin with manipulatives *(pattern or attribute blocks, colored disks, etc.).*

Using the Chart

1. Show Chart 9.

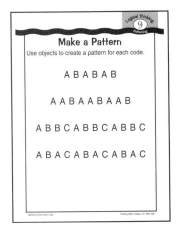

2. Read the pattern code.

3. Have students make a pattern that matches the code with real objects.

4. Then record the patterns on the chalkboard or chart paper.

5. As your students are ready, have small groups or individuals produce their own patterns and share them with the class.

Practicing the Skill

Students complete the activity page, *Make Your Own Pattern,* on page 77.

Extending the Skill

Challenge students to create their own patterns with multicode names.

Click and drag the objects at the top of the chart into patterns after students have created their "real" patterns.

Thinking Skills, Grades 1–2 • EMC 5301

Make a Pattern

Use objects to create a pattern for each code.

A B A B A B

A A B A A B A A B

A B B C A B B C A B B C

A B A C A B A C A B A C

Make Your Own Pattern

Create a pattern for each code.

A B B A B B A B B

A A B C A A B C A A B C

A A B B C A A B B C A A B B C

How Many Legs?

Introducing the Skill

1. Help students solve problems using patterns that they have identified. Pose this question:

   How many eyes, in all, do five people have?

2. Allow students to solve the problem independently and to explain how they came to the conclusions that they did.

3. Then make this chart.

   One person has _____ eyes.

   Two people have _____ eyes.

   Three people have _____ eyes.

   Four people have _____ eyes.

   Five people have _____ eyes.

4. Have students write the number of eyes in each blank. Ask:

   Is there a pattern?
   2, 4, 6, 8, 10—counting by 2s

   How could this pattern help us solve problems?

   We could count by 2s to answer how many eyes 7 or 15 people have.

Using the Chart

1. Show Chart 10.

2. Ask students how many legs there are in each row, and fill in the boxes. Then ask students to identify the pattern made by the numbers in the boxes.

3. Circle the numbers at the bottom of the chart to continue the pattern.

4. Answer the question: *How many legs do eight cows have?*

Practicing the Skill

Students complete the activity page, *How Many Fingers?*, on page 80.

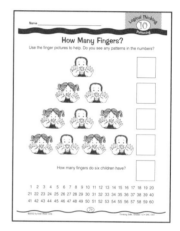

Extending the Skill

Have students write an original problem that could be solved using a pattern. As a class, try solving some of these problems.

Keyboard numbers in each box to tell how many you saw. Then click on the multiples of 4 to change the numbers to red.

78

How Many Legs?

How many legs do eight cows have?

Use the cow pictures to help. Do you see any patterns in the numbers?

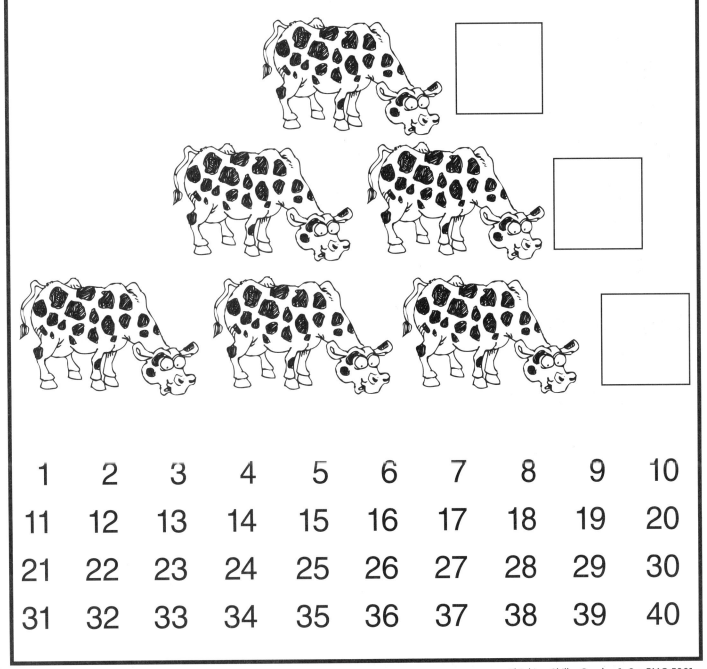

1	2	3	4	5	6	7	8	9	10
11	12	13	14	15	16	17	18	19	20
21	22	23	24	25	26	27	28	29	30
31	32	33	34	35	36	37	38	39	40

Name _____

How Many Fingers?

Use the finger pictures to help. Do you see any patterns in the numbers?

How many fingers do six children have?

1   2   3   4   5   6   7   8   9   10   11   12   13   14   15   16   17   18   19   20
21 22 23 24 25 26 27 28 29 30 31 32 33 34 35 36 37 38 39 40
41 42 43 44 45 46 47 48 49 50 51 52 53 54 55 56 57 58 59 60

80

Thinking Skills, Grades 1–2 • EMC 5301

A-1 Hairstyles

Introducing the Skill

This chart is more difficult because the A-1 hairstyles have two factors in common. Both factors must be present to qualify a hairstyle as A-1.

Using the Chart

1. Show Chart 11.

2. Ask students to describe each of the three A-1 hairstyles.

   What is the same about each one?

   What makes an A-1 hairstyle? (curls and at least one bow)

3. Discuss why each of the other three styles is not an A-1 hairstyle.

   (one has no bow, one has no curls, one has neither curls nor bow)

4. Have students draw an A-1 hairstyle.

Practicing the Skill

Students complete the activity page, *Speedster,* on page 83.

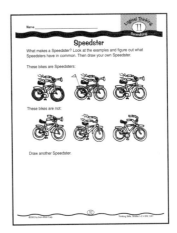

Extending the Skill

Challenge students to draw several speedsters that have the required attributes, but that are different in other ways.

Click and drag the elements to the head to create an A-1 hairstyle.

Thinking Skills, Grades 1–2 • EMC 5301

A-1 Hairstyles

What makes an A-1 hairstyle?

These are A-1 hairstyles:

These are not:

Give this face an
A-1 hairstyle.

Speedster

What makes a Speedster? Look at the examples and figure out what Speedsters have in common. Then draw your own Speedster.

These bikes are Speedsters:

These bikes are not:

Draw another Speedster.

Thinking Skills, Grades 1–2 • EMC 5301

Twinkles

Introducing the Skill

Creating puzzles is a precise activity. The Twinkles puzzle has added distracters *(eyes, smiles)*. Students must carefully check to see that they haven't inadvertently added or left out a definitive feature as they analyze their sets.

Using the Chart

1. Show Chart 12.

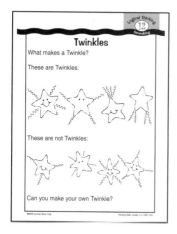

2. Read the chart together and, if you feel they are ready, divide your class into small groups to solve the puzzle. Require that groups be able to explain their solutions.

3. Have each student draw a Twinkle.

Practicing the Skill

Students complete the activity page, *Swingers*, on page 86.

Extending the Skill

Have students create their own puzzles.

Name a thing and list its attributes.

Draw three examples of the thing.

Draw three examples that are not the thing.

Click and drag the elements to create a Twinkle.

Twinkles

What makes a Twinkle?

These are Twinkles:

These are not Twinkles:

Can you make your own Twinkle?

Swingers

What makes a Swinger? Look at the examples and figure out what Swingers have in common. Then draw your own Swinger.

These are Swingers:

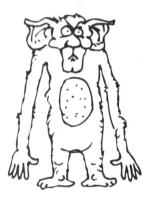 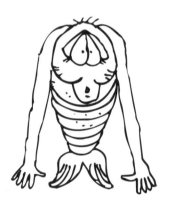 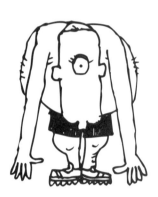

These are not:

Draw a Swinger.

86

Look Again!

Introducing the Skill

The word *analysis* is derived from a Greek word meaning "to divide into parts," or "to dissolve." Analysis is the act of separating a whole into parts. Help your students divide this puzzle into parts, seeing it in many different ways.

Using the Chart

1. Show Chart 13.

2. Trace around triangles with a colored erasable pen.

3. Have students keep a tally of the triangles as they are marked.

4. Share strategies for "seeing" the triangle in different ways. It may help students to have several copies of the chart. On one chart they could number the small triangles. On another they could outline and number larger ones.

Practicing the Skill

Students complete the activity page, *Everywhere Square,* on page 89.

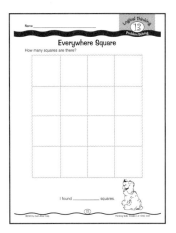

Extending the Skill

Have students build composite shapes with square blocks and count the number of squares they create. Transfer the shapes to graph paper.

Click on the different-sized triangles to highlight them in the puzzle. Then keyboard numbers in each box to tell how many you saw.

Thinking Skills, Grades 1–2 • EMC 5301

Look Again!

How many triangles can you find?

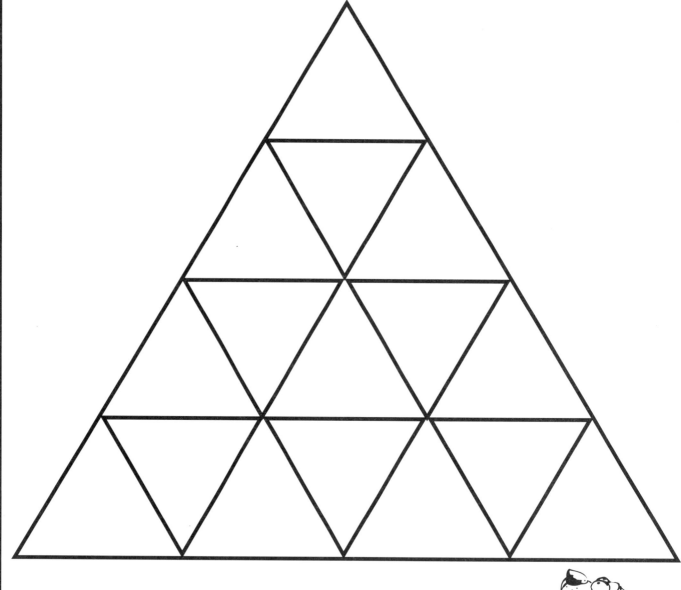

Everywhere Square

How many squares are there?

I found _____ squares.

Thinking Skills, Grades 1–2 • EMC 5301

Heat It Up

Introducing the Skill

This exercise asks students to infer the effect of heat or cold on different objects. Discuss examples of the effects that heat and cold have had on things within students' prior experiences.

ice cube on a hot day

VCR tape left in a hot car

dog's water dish left outside in the winter

food in the freezer

Using the Chart

1. Show Chart 14.

2. Ask students to infer the effect of heat on each object.

3. Ask questions such as:

   Do the objects change form?

   Is the change permanent?

   Can you see, feel, hear, and smell the change?

Practicing the Skill

Students complete the activity page, *Freeze It,* on page 92.

Extending the Skill

Have students infer the effect of cold on each object on Chart 14.

Click in each box and keyboard responses.
Click on images to see possible changes.

Thinking Skills, Grades 1–2 • EMC 5301

Heat It Up

What would happen if you heated each of these things in the oven?

Name _____

Freeze It

What would happen if you placed each of these things in the freezer overnight? Tell or write your ideas.

Thinking Skills, Grades 1–2 • EMC 5301

Critical Thinking

©2002 by Evan-Moor Corp.

Thinking Skills, Grades 1–2 • EMC 5301

Sorting the Groceries

Introducing the Skill

1. Introduce the idea of **sorting** to classify. Show students a set of familiar classroom supplies. For example:

   scissors, pencil, paper, paints, brush, counters, math flash cards, playground ball, jump rope, and pipe cleaners

2. Have students sort the items into groups. Give them the rules or attributes for sorting.

   Sort the supplies into three groups: items for art, items for math, and items for P.E.

Using the Chart

1. Show Chart 1.

2. Record the way the groceries are sorted.

Practicing the Skill

Students complete the activity page, *Whose Is It?*, on page 96. They cut and paste to sort clothing and accessories.

Extending the Skill

Have students sort additional sets of familiar objects.

- Library books—real, make-believe

- Coat rack—zippered coats, buttoned coats

Click on the object to see which category it represents.

Milk—You drink me.

Sponges—You clean with me.

Juice—You drink me.

Bread—You eat me.

Soap—You clean with me.

Carrots—You eat me.

Cereal—You eat me.

Cookies—You eat me.

94

Sorting the Groceries

- Tell which ones you will eat.

- Tell which ones you will drink.

- Tell which ones will help you clean.

Name _____

Whose Is It?

Sort the clothes. Paste each item under its owner.

Mom	Tommy	Baby Sister

Thinking Skills, Grades 1–2 • EMC 5301

How Will You Group Them?

Introducing the Skill

1. Have students describe the process of sorting objects into groups.

2. Model the process of identifying criteria, or "rules" for sorting.

   - Show students several boxes of cereal. Think of different ways the cereals could be classified. For example:

     big boxes   *little boxes*
     round cereal   *square cereal*
     sugar-coated cereal   *no-sugar cereal*
     cereal I like   *cereal I don't like*

   - Then sort the cereals.

3. Make sure that students recognize that there are many correct categories for sorting the cereals.

Using the Chart

1. Show Chart 2.

2. Challenge students to identify rules for sorting and then to sort the animals according to the rules.

3. Have students explain their rules. Note the different rules that have been used.

Practicing the Skill

Challenge students to identify their own rules for sorting as they complete the activity page, *Clarisa's Closet,* on page 99.

Extending the Skill

Have students sort the same group of objects in several different ways. Be sure that they can explain their sorting rules.

Click and drag the animals into groups.

Thinking Skills, Grades 1–2 • EMC 5301

How Will You Group Them?

Sort the animals into groups.

Tell what rules you used to group them.

Clarisa's Closet

Help Clarisa organize the items in her closet.

Cut out the pictures and put them neatly in the closet.

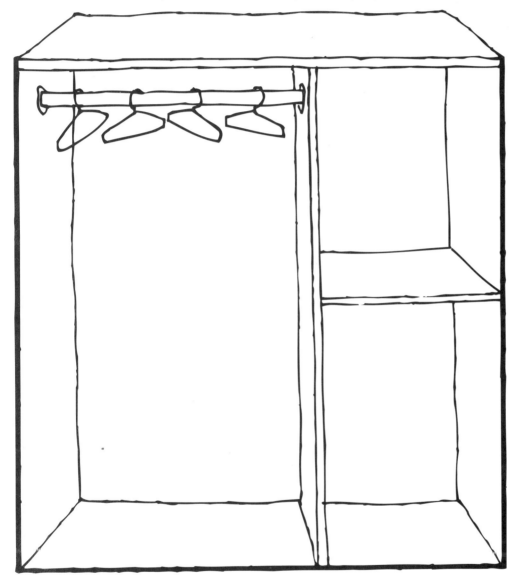

Tell what rule you used for organizing them.

_____

_____

_____

Find the Twins

Introducing the Skill

1. Have students explain the words *exactly alike.*

2. Show students six pencils—two should be exactly alike, the others should be different in at least one way.

3. Have students describe how the pencils are alike. Students indicate the "twin" pencils as the two that are exactly alike.

4. Explain that when you are looking for similarities you are comparing things.

Using the Chart

1. Show Chart 3.

2. Have students describe the similarities between the dogs on the chart.

3. Identify the "twin" dogs.

Practicing the Skill

Students complete the activity page, *Find the Twins,* on page 102.

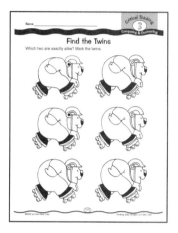

Extending the Skill

1. Have students draw a set of balls that are the same shape and size.

2. Students color two of the balls with the same colors and the same patterns. They color the other balls differently in at least one way.

3. Post the sets and challenge students to identify the "twins."

Drag an *X* onto each of the twins.

Thinking Skills, Grades 1–2 • EMC 5301

Find the Twins

Which two pictures are exactly alike?

Mark the twins.

Find the Twins

Which two are exactly alike? Mark the twins.

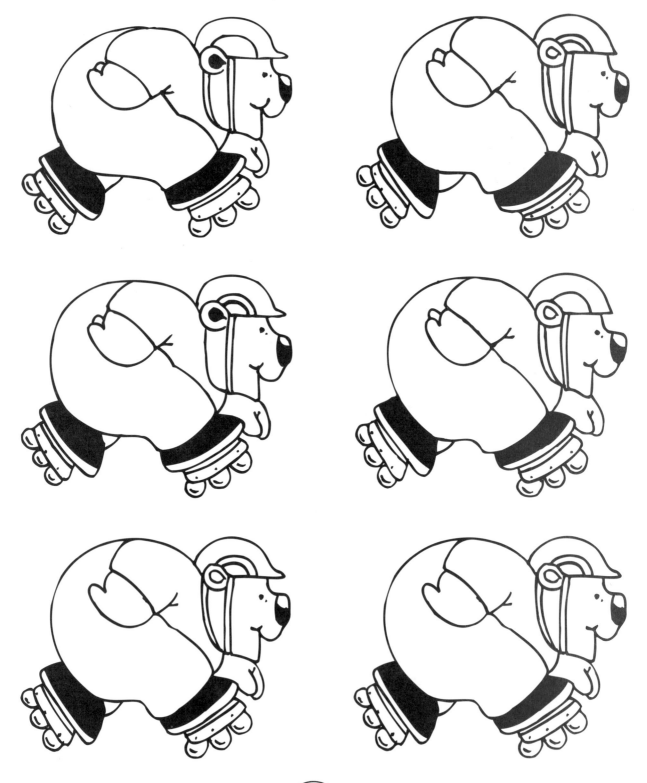

What's the Difference?

Introducing the Skill

1. Show students two books. Have them identify the ways that the two books are different.

   size, shape, color, thickness, subject, age, etc.

2. Record the differences.

3. Explain that when you look for differences it is called **contrasting**.

Using the Chart

1. Show Chart 4.

2. Have students name the differences they see in the two wagons.

3. List the differences on the chalkboard or a chart.

Practicing the Skill

Students complete the activity page, *What's the Difference?*, on page 105.

Extending the Skill

1. Provide simple pictures of objects for students to trace.

2. Students start with two identical tracings and add several identical features. Then they add several different features.

3. Share the drawings and determine the differences.

Click in the text box and keyboard the differences.

Thinking Skills, Grades 1–2 • EMC 5301

What's the Difference?

The wagons are different in many ways.

Can you find them all?

What's the Difference?

The hats are different in at least eight ways. Tell a friend about the differences you see. Did you find all eight?

Draw a new hat. Make it like each of the other hats in four ways.

Thinking Skills, Grades 1–2 • EMC 5301

A Rag Doll and a Puppy

Introducing the Skill

1. Explain that any two items can have similarities and differences.

2. Show two very different objects and have your class compare the two. Examples:

a rubber boot	*a book jacket*
a flag	*a pansy*
a globe	*a phone book*

Using the Chart

1. Show Chart 5.

2. Encourage students to think beyond the obvious as they compare and contrast the rag doll and the puppy.

3. Record student responses. Often their responses are insightful and eloquent.

Practicing the Skill

1. Students complete the activity page, *Chocolate Chip Cookies and the Moon,* on page 108.

2. Take time to share student responses.

Extending the Skill

Have students bring two things from home for a comparison exercise. Each student writes or tells about another student's objects.

Click in the text box and keyboard students' responses.

A Rag Doll and a Puppy

Compare a rag doll and a puppy.

- Tell how they are alike.

- Tell how they are different.

Name _____

Chocolate Chip Cookies and the Moon

Compare a chocolate chip cookie and the moon.

Tell how they are alike.

_____

_____

_____

Tell how they are different.

_____

_____

_____

108

K-9s

Introducing the Skill

1. Review the terms **similarities** and **differences**.

2. Remind students that when they sorted objects, they identified a characteristic or attribute that objects had in common. This logic riddle takes sorting one step further. Students will identify an attribute that members of a group have and then create a new member of the group that has the same attribute.

Using the Chart

1. Show Chart 6.

2. Develop a strategy for solving these problems by identifying the similarities and differences. Say:

   What do all the K-9s have in common?

   Identify which characteristic is absent in each of the "not K-9s."

3. Draw a new member of the K-9s. Make sure that the common characteristic is included.

4. Have each student draw a K-9.

5. Share the drawings. Check to make sure that the common characteristics have been included.

Practicing the Skill

Students complete the activity page, *Super Pets,* on page 111.

Click on the dogs that are <u>not</u> K-9s to find out why they aren't.

First dog—I don't have a tag.

Second dog—I don't have a collar or a tag.

Third dog—I don't have a collar.

K-9s

What makes a K-9? Look at the examples and figure out what the K-9s have in common. Then draw your own K-9.

These dogs are K-9s:

These dogs are not:

Super Pets

What makes a Super Pet? Look at the examples and figure out what Super Pets have in common. Then draw your own Super Pet.

These pets are Super Pets:

These pets are not:

Draw another Super Pet.

Thinking Skills, Grades 1–2 • EMC 5301

What Will Happen?

Introducing the Skill

Observing the world with focused attention develops the ability to study everyday objects—plants, clothes, a sidewalk—and discover new ideas. Precise observation is an important skill that requires practice to develop.

Using the Chart

1. Show Chart 7.

2. Read the question.

3. List student responses/predictions without judgment.

   It will get wet.
   It will sink.
   It will float.
   It will land on the bottom.
   It will weigh more.

4. Set up the activity and gather students so that all can view what happens. Call on a student to place the cloth in the water. Read each prediction and evaluate its correctness. Cross out those that are not observable. Add any new observations.

Practicing the Skill

Students complete the activity page, *Different Changes,* on page 114. If your class is not writing fluently, you may wish to do the activity in small groups with a parent or cross-age tutor acting as recorder.

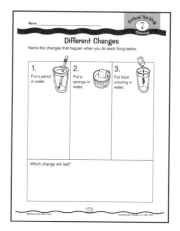

Extending the Skill

Ask students to think about whether the changes they observed in the practice activity would be lasting changes or temporary changes.

Click in the text box and keyboard students' responses.

Thinking Skills, Grades 1–2 • EMC 5301

What Will Happen?

What happens when you put a cloth in water?

Tell what you think. Then try it. Name at least three changes you observed.

Different Changes

Name the changes that happen when you do each thing below.

1.

Put a pencil in water.

2.

Put a sponge in water.

3.

Put food coloring in water.

Which change will last?

Thinking Skills, Grades 1–2 • EMC 5301

Using Your Five Senses

Introducing the Skill

Provide real balloons for the activity on Chart 8. Read over the chart directions before passing out the balloons.

Using the Chart

1. Show Chart 8.

2. Talk about what students observe as each step is experienced. Guide students to tell about their observations using all five senses.

3. Record the class's observations by the sense used.

   Example:

   Sound—The rubber squeaks. The end snaps when I pull it.

   Sight—It's getting bigger. The color is getting lighter.

Practicing the Skill

1. Give students a pile of assorted leaves for the leaf activity. Make sure that the leaves are safe to taste. Warn students not to taste leaves outside the classroom unless an adult approves the leaves first.

2. Students complete the activity page, *Using Your Senses,* on page 117.

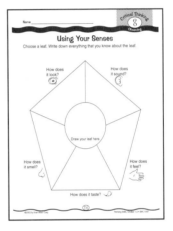

Extending the Skill

Using observations made with their five senses, have students write about a familiar object. Share the descriptions and see if other students can guess what is being described.

Click on the balloon and watch it get bigger with each click. Then keyboard the description in the text box.

Thinking Skills, Grades 1–2 • EMC 5301

Using Your Five Senses

Look at a balloon.

- Feel it.

- Stretch it.

- Blow it up a little.

- Describe what you observe.

- How is the balloon changing?

- Continue blowing.

- Make observations.

- Tell what happens.

Using Your Senses

Choose a leaf. Write down everything that you know about the leaf.

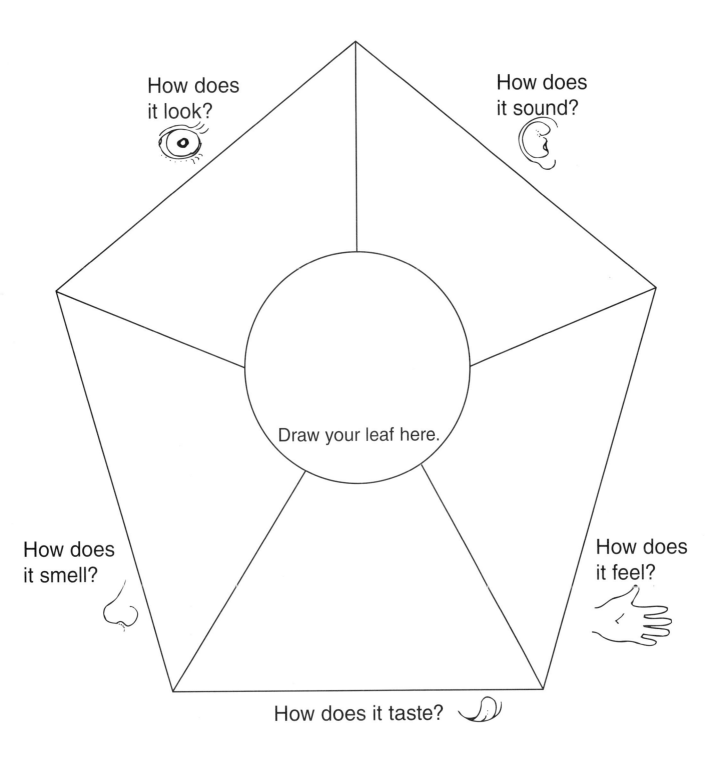

How does
it look?

How does
it sound?

Draw your leaf here.

How does
it smell?

How does
it feel?

How does it taste?

Thinking Skills, Grades 1–2 • EMC 5301

An Apple

Introducing the Skill

Using an observation mat like the one pictured on Chart 9 encourages the use of all the senses when describing an object. Create a copy of the chart on the chalkboard or a large sheet of butcher paper, or make a transparency of Chart 9.

Using the Chart

1. Give each student several apple slices. Use several kinds of apples to maximize the variety of descriptions.

2. Show Chart 9.

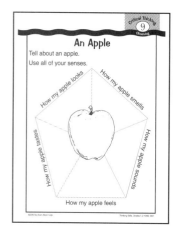

3. Ask students to describe the apple slices. Depending on the oral language levels of your students, you may need to do substantial guiding to generate interesting descriptions.

4. Record their descriptions on the chart you have prepared.

Practicing the Skill

Students complete the activity page, *Part of My Lunch,* on page 120.

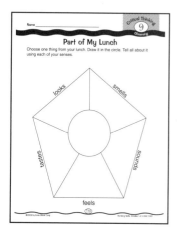

Extending the Skill

Summarize the observations by writing a descriptive paragraph about the apple.

Click in each text box to record students' responses.

An Apple

Tell about an apple.

Use all of your senses.

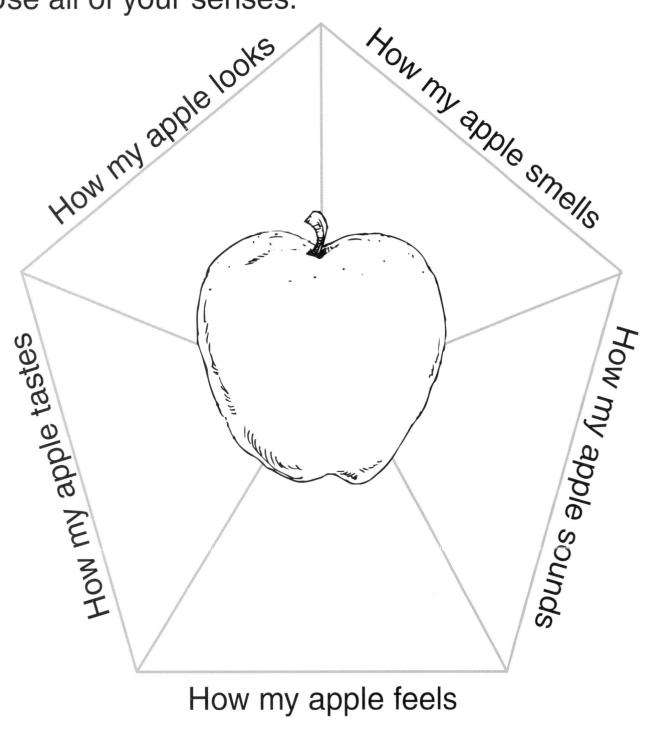

How my apple looks

How my apple smells

How my apple tastes

How my apple sounds

How my apple feels

Part of My Lunch

Choose one thing from your lunch. Draw it in the circle. Tell all about it using each of your senses.

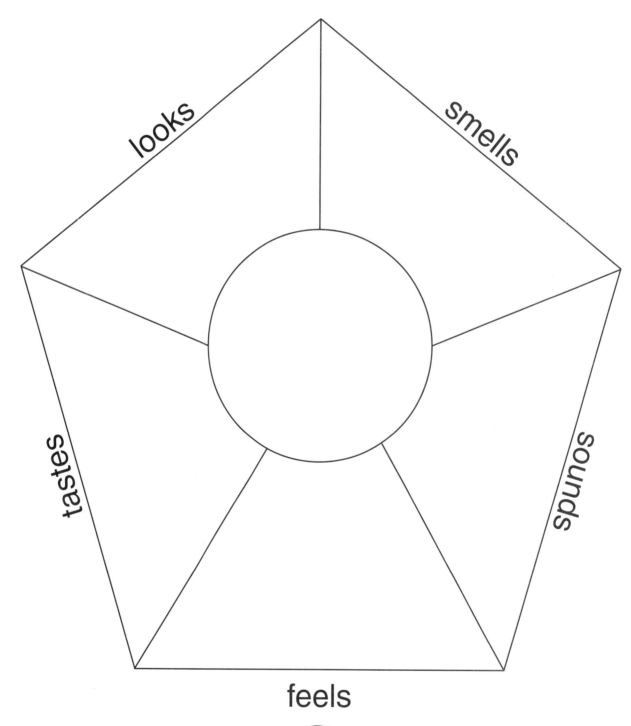

looks

smells

tastes

sounds

feels

Largest to Smallest

Introducing the Skill

1. Practice putting real things in order before you begin the symbolic work on the chart and activity sheet. Show students four different-sized pencils.

2. Ask students to place the pencils in order from longest to shortest.

3. Repeat using different objects *(students, books, balls, desks)* and different attributes for ordering the objects.

Using the Chart

1. Show Chart 10.

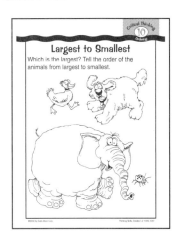

2. Guide students to state that they are placing the animals in order by size.

3. Students order the animals.

4. Ask students if there is a different way to order the animals. *(length, weight, height)* Place the animals in order in the new ways suggested.

Practicing the Skill

Students complete the activity page, *Oldest to Youngest,* on page 123.

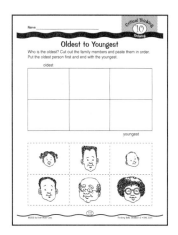

Extending the Skill

Have each student choose four objects and an attribute to use in ordering the objects. Set up a center where students practice putting things in order.

Click and drag the animals into line.

(121)

Largest to Smallest

Which is the largest? Tell the order of the animals from largest to smallest.

Oldest to Youngest

Who is the oldest? Cut out the family members and paste them in order.
Put the oldest person first and end with the youngest.

oldest

youngest

123

How Did It Happen?

Introducing the Skill

Discuss your students' first experiences with their bicycles.

Using the Chart

1. Show Chart 11.

2. Guide students to state that they are ordering the pictures to show which happened first.

3. As a group, students order the pictures.

4. Have students explain the reason that they ordered the pictures the way they did.

Practicing the Skill

Students complete the activity page, *Building a Birdhouse,* on page 126.

Extending the Skill

Have students write and illustrate a story about their first experience with a bike.

Click in each circle and keyboard the correct number.

(124)

How Did It Happen?

Number the pictures in order to show what happened when Tommy rode his new bike.

Building a Birdhouse

Paste the pictures in order to show how Eric built a birdhouse. Then write the story that the pictures tell.

_____

_____

_____

_____

Thinking Skills, Grades 1–2 • EMC 5301

Striped Things, Square Things

Introducing the Skill

Venn diagrams are an important visual tool for grouping items that are alike and different. If your class has no experience with Venn diagrams, introduce this tool before doing this lesson.

1. Make large overlapping circles of string or rope on the floor. Label one circle "Boys" and the other circle "Students with High-top Shoes."

2. Say, *"All the things in the first circle are boys, and all the things in the second circle are students with high-top shoes."*

3. Choose a boy without high-tops and ask, *"Where should _____ stand?"*

4. When that boy is placed in the "Boy" circle, choose a girl with high-top shoes. Ask, *"Where should _____ stand?"*

5. Continue placing boys without high-tops and girls with high-tops. Then choose a boy with high-tops.

   Ask, *"Where should _____ stand?"* *(The boy must stand in both circles. He is a boy and a student with high-tops, so place him in the section where the two circles overlap, the intersection of the two sets.)*

6. Ask, *"What about a girl with sandals?"* *(She must stand outside the two circles, because she is neither a boy nor a student with high-top shoes.)*

Using the Chart

1. Show Chart 12.

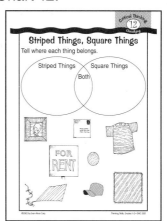

2. Make sure that students understand the labels on the Venn diagram.

3. Students place each item on the chart in the appropriate section.

4. Ask students to explain why they placed items as they did.

Practicing the Skill

Students complete the activity page, *Cookies,* on page 129.

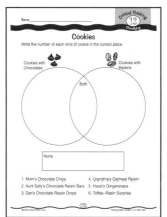

Click and drag objects into the Venn diagram.

Thinking Skills, Grades 1–2 • EMC 5301

Striped Things, Square Things

Tell where each thing belongs.

Striped Things | Square Things

Both

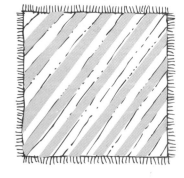
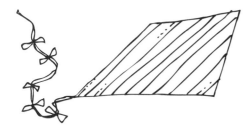

Cookies

Write the number of each kind of cookie in the correct place.

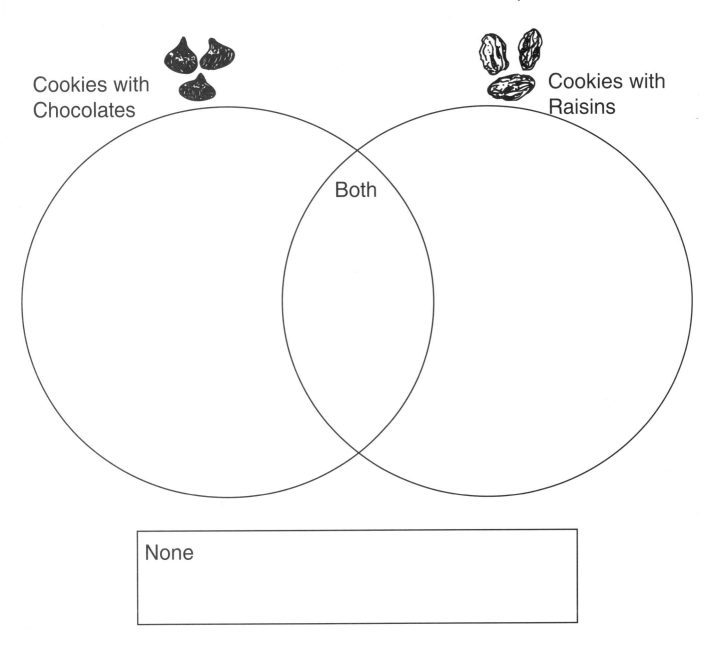

Cookies with
Chocolates

Cookies with
Raisins

Both

None

1. Mom's Chocolate Chips

2. Aunt Sally's Chocolate Raisin Bars

3. Dan's Chocolate Raisin Drops

4. Grandma's Oatmeal Raisin

5. Hazel's Gingersnaps

6. Toffee-Raisin Surprise

129

Puppies, Puppies, Puppies

Introducing the Skill

Discuss and label the intersecting areas of the three circles on the Venn diagram to help your students see what combinations of attributes are being grouped together.

Using the Chart

1. Show Chart 13.

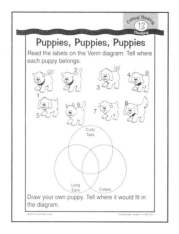

2. Make sure that students understand the attributes stated in the Venn diagram.

3. Students write each puppy's number in the appropriate section on the diagram.

4. Have students explain why they placed the puppies as they did.

Practicing the Skill

Students complete the activity page, *Balls, Balls, Balls,* on page 132.

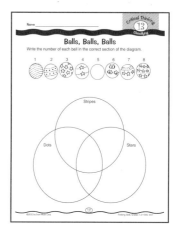

Extending the Skill

Use Venn diagrams for tracking assignments in your classroom—*spelling completed, math completed, book report turned in.* Students will put their names in a set to indicate what work they have completed.

Drag the puppies to the place they belong.

Puppies, Puppies, Puppies

Read the labels on the Venn diagram. Tell where each puppy belongs.

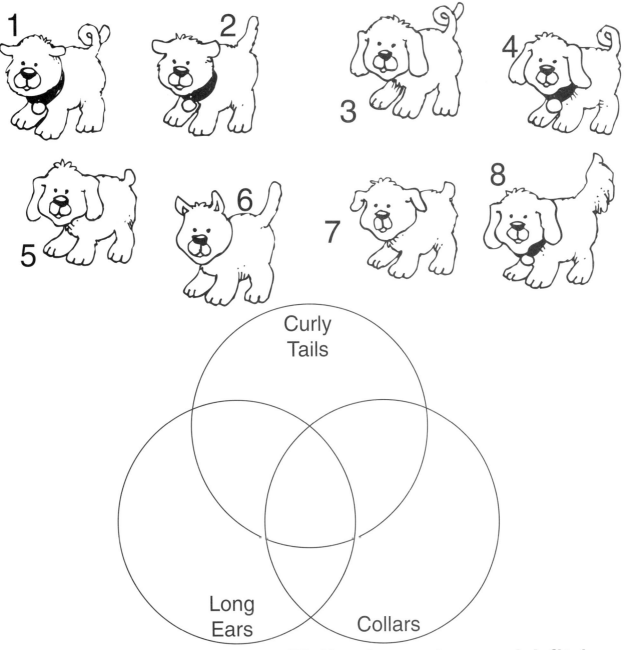

Draw your own puppy. Tell where it would fit in the diagram.

Balls, Balls, Balls

Write the number of each ball in the correct section of the diagram.

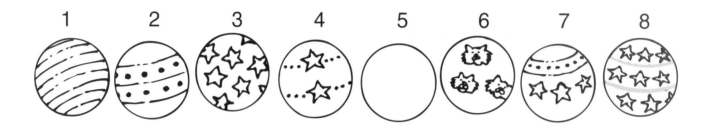

1   2   3   4   5   6   7   8

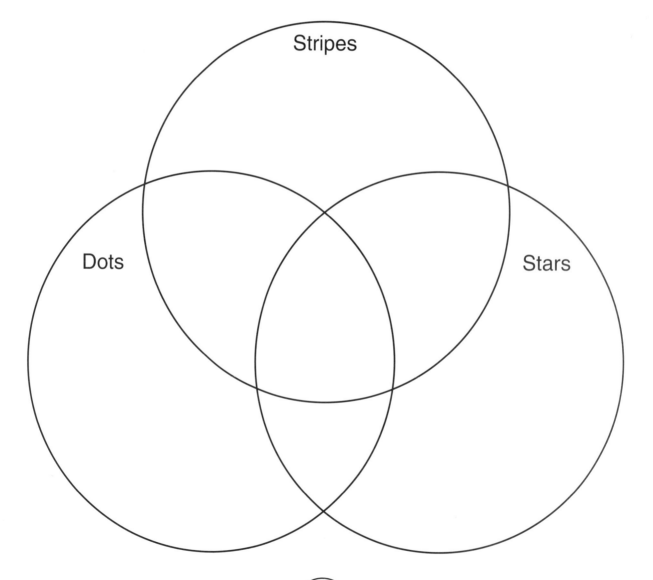

Stripes

Dots

Stars

Thinking Skills, Grades 1–2 • EMC 5301

Which Wheels for You?

Introducing the Skill

Students must interpret the information they are given to identify the attributes used to place the individuals and groups of people in this Venn diagram. Explain to your students that the diagram they will be completing today is more complicated than the ones they have done before, because the information that they need is "hidden" in the sentences. It is their job to find the information and then complete the diagram.

Using the Chart

1. Show Chart 14.

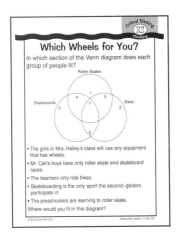

2. Read the labels on the diagram. Make sure that students understand each label. Talk about the intersecting sections and what combinations of attributes would be shared in each one.

3. Read the sentences together and discuss where to place each group.

Practicing the Skill

Students complete the activity page, *Favorite Subjects,* on page 135.

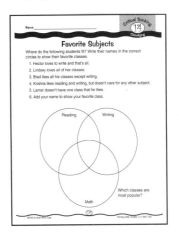

Extending the Skill

Venn diagrams can help classify groups of people or objects so that the data can be analyzed in a visual way. After you have classified each group of students from the chart, have your students interpret the diagram. Ask:

Which wheels are used the most?

Which wheels are used the least?

Why would this information be important to know?

Click and drag numbers to show where each group would be in the diagram.

Which Wheels for You?

In which section of the Venn diagram does each group of people fit?

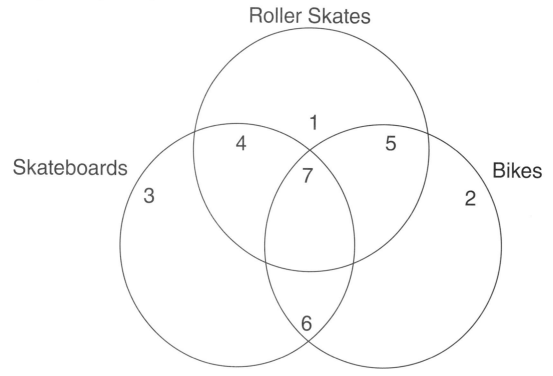

Roller Skates

Skateboards

Bikes

1

4

5

7

3

2

6

- The girls in Mrs. Halley's class will use any equipment that has wheels.

- Mr. Call's boys have only roller skate and skateboard races.

- The teachers ride only bikes.

- Skateboarding is the only sport the second-graders participate in.

- The preschoolers are learning to roller skate.

Where would you fit in this diagram?

Favorite Subjects

Where do the following students fit? Write their names in the correct circles to show their favorite classes.

1. Hector loves to write and that's all.

2. Lindsey loves all of her classes.

3. Brad likes all his classes except writing.

4. Krishna likes reading and writing, but doesn't care for any other subject.

5. Lamar doesn't have one class that he likes.

6. Add your name to show your favorite class.

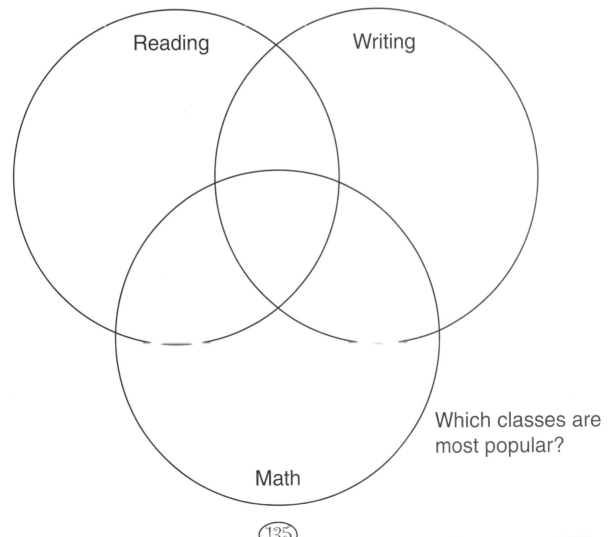

Reading   Writing

Math

Which classes are most popular?

    Thinking Skills, Grades 1–2 • EMC 5301

A Riddle

Introducing the Skill

1. Have students tell what it means to compare two things.

2. Explain that not only objects, but also words can be compared. This activity will compare words.

Using the Chart

1. Show Chart 15.

A Riddle

Critical Thinking
15
Compare and Contrast

Solve the word puzzle to answer this riddle:
They fill pillows and parkas
And helped George Washington write.
They take to the air
And help birds in flight.

Column A	Column B
a place where crops are grown	what you put in a sleeve
a contest between runners	a vehicle
what you wear when it's cold outside	a portable bed
a shelter for campers	pennies in a dime
Your ears help you _____	An elephant can flap its _____
where you sit	Jack Horner _____ in the corner
to fall from a high position	Peas grow in a _____
the actors in a play	a grown-up kitten

©2002 by Evan-Moor Corp.   Thinking Skills, Grades 1-2 • EMC 5301

2. Explain the directions for solving the word puzzle.

   • *Write a word in the blanks in Column A that means the same as the words given. The word must have four letters.*

   • *Complete Column B in the same way. Answers in Column B must have three letters.*

   • *Compare the word in Column A with the word in Column B. Find the one letter that is different.*

   • *Write the extra letter in the box between the two columns.*

   • *When you're done, read the word down the middle that solves the puzzle.*

Practicing the Skill

Students complete the activity page, *Strings and Keys,* on page 138.

Name _____

Critical Thinking
15
Compare and Contrast

Strings and Keys
• Write words that answer the clues.
• Write the extra letter from each Column A word in the box.
• Read down the boxes to find something that uses keys and strings to bring us pleasure.

Column A	Column B
a small quantity of water	a fishing pole
bucket	a good friend
a group that plays a sport together	I _____ my friend at 2:00.
ripped	old food will do this
floating vehicle	used to hit a ball

©2002 by Evan-Moor Corp.   Thinking Skills, Grades 1-2 • EMC 5301

CD Tips

Click under each clue and keyboard the answer. Then keyboard the extra letter in the center square. Click on the answer button to see the answer to the puzzle.

A Riddle

Solve the word puzzle to answer this riddle:

> They fill pillows and parkas
> And helped George Washington write.
> They take to the air
> And help birds in flight.

Column A		Column B
a place where crops are grown		what you put in a sleeve
a contest between runners		a vehicle
what you wear when it's cold outside		a portable bed
a shelter for campers		pennies in a dime
Your ears help you _____.		An elephant can flap its _____.
where you sit		Jack Horner _____ in the corner.
to fall from a high position		Peas grow in a _____.
the actors in a play		a grown-up kitten

Strings and Keys

- Write words that answer the clues.

- Write the extra letter from each Column A word in the box.

- Read down the boxes to find something that uses keys and strings to bring us pleasure.

Column A		Column B
a small quantity of water __ __ __ __ __		a fishing pole __ __ __
bucket __ __ __ __ __ __		a good friend __ __ __
a group that plays a sport together __ __ __ __ __		I _____ my friend at 2:00. __ __ __ __ __
ripped __ __ __ __ __ __		old food will do this __ __ __ __
floating vehicle __ __ __ __ __		used to hit a ball __ __ __

Answer Key

Creative Thinking

Chart 1
Answers will vary.

Activity Page 7
Answers will vary.

Chart 2
Answers will vary.

Activity Page 10
Answers will vary.

Chart 3
Answers will vary.

Activity Page 13
Answers will vary.

Chart 4
There are four possible bouquets: tulip, daisy, iris; tulip, lily, iris; daisy, lily, iris; tulip, daisy, lily.

Activity Page 16
red, blue, purple, green; blue, purple, green, orange; purple, green, orange, yellow; green, orange, yellow, red; orange, yellow, red, blue; yellow, red, blue, purple

Chart 5
Accept any reasonable response.

Activity Page 19
Answers will vary.

Chart 6
Answers may include: A spoon scoops, measures, stirs, and strains.

Activity Page 22
Answers will vary.

Chart 7
Most possible: 5

Activity Page 25
Most possible: 5

Chart 8
Answers will vary.

Activity Page 28
Ideas will vary.

Chart 9
Stories will vary.

Activity Page 31
Stories will vary.

Chart 10

Activity Page 34

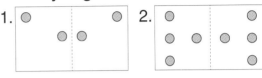

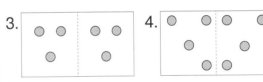

Chart 11

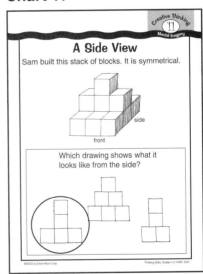

Thinking Skills, Grades 1–2 • EMC 5301

Activity Page 37

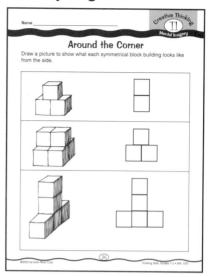

Chart 12

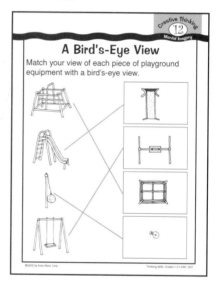

Activity Page 40
Accept drawings that present a reasonable representation.

Chart 13
4D, 1C, 2C, 3D

Activity Page 43
a plate

Chart 14

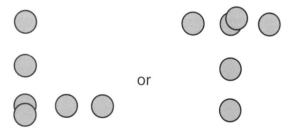

Activity Page 46

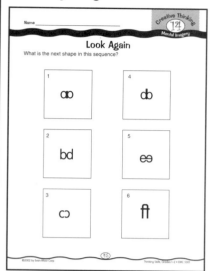

Chart 15
Ideas will vary.

Activity Page 49
Ideas will vary.

Logical Thinking

Chart 1
dog, foot, cow

Activity Page 53
cow, foot, rabbit

Chart 2
In Analogy 1 the items should be opposites. In Analogy 2 the items should be a worker and the worker's jobsite. In Analogy 3 the items should be opposites. In Analogies 4 and 5 the relationship between the items may vary.

Activity Page 56
Answers may vary.

Chart 3
Sara, canary; Susie, puppy; Sally, kitten; Sam, lizard; Sean, goat

Activity Page 59
Paul, hamburger; Karina, pizza; Tomas, salad; Max, soup

Chart 4
Andre, Tuesday; Kim, Monday; Steve, Thursday; Maya, Wednesday; Carlos, Friday

Activity Page 62
Dad, lion; Mom, giraffe; Tenisha, monkey; Jamal, elephant

Chart 5

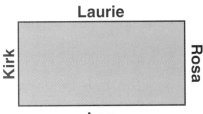

Positions may be rotated, but sequence must be as shown.

Activity Page 65

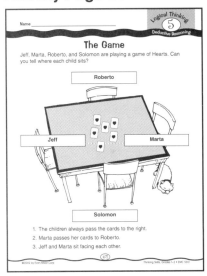

Positions may be rotated, but sequence must be as shown.

Chart 6

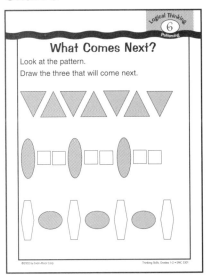

Activity Page 68
ball, ball, frisbee; skateboard, roller blade, skateboard; bat, ball, bat, ball, bat, mitt

Chart 7
ABABABA; AABAABAA; AAABAAABA; ABCABCABCABCABC

Activity Page 71

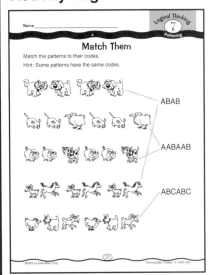

Chart 8
tall, short, tall, short; party, ball, party, fedora, party, ball, party, fedora; striped, striped, plain, plain, striped, striped, plain, plain; tassel, no tassel, tassel, no tassel; bear, no bear, bear, no bear

Activity Page 74
lock on top, lock in front, no lock, lock on top, lock in front, no lock; rectangle, curved top, round & soft, rectangle, curved top, round & soft; colored, white, colored, colored, white, colored; square handle, square handle, round handle, square handle, square handle, round handle; name, no name, no name, name, no name, no name

Chart 9
Arrangement of objects or drawings must show each of the four patterns on the chart.

Activity Page 77
Pictures will vary.

Chart 10
8 cows have 32 feet, count by 4s

Activity Page 80
One child has 10 fingers. Two children have 20 fingers. Three children have 30 fingers. Four children have 40 fingers. Six children have 60 fingers.

Chart 11
An A-1 hairstyle must have curls and a bow.

Activity Page 83
A Speedster must have a horn and streamers.

Chart 12
A Twinkle must have five points and four squiggly lines.

Activity Page 86
A Swinger must have two long arms.

Chart 13
27 triangles

Activity Page 89
30 squares

Chart 14
Accept reasonable responses; encourage creative ideas.

Activity Page 92
Accept reasonable responses.

Critical Thinking

Chart 1
Eat: cookies, carrots, bread, cereal; **Drink:** milk, juice; **Clean:** sponges, soap

Activity Page 96
Mom: dress, skirt, purse; **Tommy:** soccer shirt, socks, shorts; **Baby:** bib, pajamas, baby shoes

Chart 2
Sorting criteria will vary, but may include differences in where animals live, how they move, number of legs, etc.

Activity Page 99
Answers will vary. Clothing may be organized by type or function.

Chart 3
Dog on top left and bottom right are alike.

Activity Page 102
The bottom two are exactly alike.

Chart 4
Differences include: color of tires, names of wagon, shape of handle, decoration on handle, paint job on body, height of sides, passenger, flag

Activity Page 105
price tag, shape of bill, logo/no logo, button on top, vents/no vents, color band around edge/no band, solid color/stripes, plain bill/striped bill, dark color/light color, dirty/clean, shape of hat

Chart 5
Accept any justifiable response related to function, appearance, location, composition, etc.

Activity Page 108
Accept any justifiable response related to function, appearance, location, composition, etc.

Chart 6
A K-9 is any dog with a collar and a tag.

Activity Page 111
A Super Pet must have four legs.

Chart 7
See notes on the teacher instruction page.

Activity Page 114
Answers may vary. **Pencil:** will get wet, will look bent. **Sponge:** will swell, will get wet, less water in dish. **Food coloring:** water will change color, all of the water will be the same color. Change 3 will last.

Chart 8
Answers will vary; see notes on teacher's instruction page.

Activity Page 117
Answers will vary.

Chart 9
Answers will vary.

Activity Page 120
Answers will vary.

Chart 10
elephant, dog, duck, ladybug

Activity Page 123

man, woman, larger boy, smaller boy, girl, baby

Chart 11

Students may suggest several ways to sequence the pictures. Accept any order that can be backed up by logical reasoning.

Activity Page 126

1. boy sawing
2. boy hammering
3. boy painting
4. finished birdhouse

Chart 12

striped things: ball, shirt; square things: sign, envelope; both: picture frame, scarf; outside Venn diagram: ball cap

Activity Page 129

cookies with chocolates–1; cookies with raisins–4, 6; both–2, 3; none–5

Chart 13

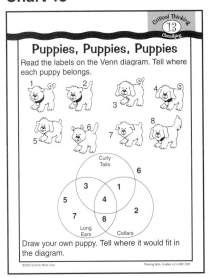

Activity Page 132

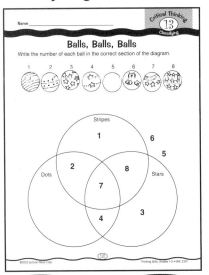

Chart 14

7–the girls in Mrs. Halley's class; 4–Mr. Call's boys; 2–the teachers; 3–second-graders; 1–preschoolers

Activity Page 135

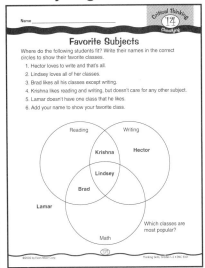

Reading and writing are the most popular classes.

Chart 15

farm	F	arm
race	E	car
coat	A	cot
tent	T	ten
hear	H	ear
seat	E	sat
drop	R	pod
cast	S	cat

Activity Page 138

drop	P	rod
pail	I	pal
team	A	met
torn	N	rot
boat	O	bat